Fire from Timbuktu,
A Dialogue with History

I0200509

Karamoh Kabba

Sierra Leonean Writers Series
(SLWS)

Fire from Timbuktu, A Dialogue with History

Copyright © 2016 by Karamoh Kabba

ISBN: 978-99910-54-35-3

Sierra Leonean Writers Series
120 Kissy Road, Freetown, Sierra Leone
Publisher: Prof. Osman Sankoh (Mallam O.)
publisher@sl-writers-series.org
www.sl-writers-series.org

Other works by the author

- *A Mother's Saga: An Account of the Rebel War in Sierra Leone,* 2003
- *Poverty amidst Gold and Diamonds i*n *With Hearts Ablaze,*
- An anthology of The International Library of Poetry
- *LION MOUNTAIN: A Perilous Evolution of the Dens,* 2004
- *Morquee: Political Drama of Wish over Wisdom, 2005*

Introduction

Fire from Timbuktu, A Dialogue with History is a revisionist history influenced by the hope of jolting new debates on Africa and its civilization.

It examines the growth and demise of an African civilization in ancient Ghana, Mali and Songhai; the role of spiritual leaders, monarchs, and the people in the developing political and economic ideals in Timbuktu. Simply, the paradoxical poverty in riches has led to a fascination with the early history of the African civilization.

A study of the roles of the kings and scholars of the Songhai and the congressional mosques of Timbuktu and Jenne has turned out empirical evidence that foreign infiltration obliterated the ancient African civilization right in its cradle, in Timbuktu, before it made any impact on the rest of the continent.

Fire from Timbuktu is also conceptualization that African civilization was parallel to Greco-Judeo-Christian Western civilization. In retrospect, Africa was a lost civilization: Timbuk-Traditionalist African civilization. With the early exposure to Islam, Christianity, and Judaism, Africa was on a springboard for a universal civilization that was bound to become Timbuk-Traditionalist-Islamic-Christian-Judeo African civilization on a unique African economic system that would have been independent of capitalism, socialism, and communism. It was entirely different from ancient hunter-gatherer communal societies as well.

1

Unlike previous studies, *Fire from Timbuktu, A Dialogue with History* is a philosophical look at Africa that offers alternative economic and political ideals for Africa in the absence of which, Africa had become a battleground for communism and capitalism and the cause of all or most of its conflicts, wars, and unsustainable economies.

Foreword

Since the treasure of human knowledge, especially in written form, there have been occasional thinkers who seek to dismantle 'accepted' narratives, especially about regions or concepts where an alternative doesn't seem to 'exist.' Usually, among conformists, such explosive narratives are ganged up against and quickly thrown out as soon as they make entry into mainstream discourse. Whether, in the end, these works are incorporated into the 'cannons' or not, depends on the weight of their arguments. But it is assuring to note that the philosopher, John Searle argued that "In my experience there never was, in fact, a fixed 'canon'; there was rather a certain set of tentative judgments about what had importance and quality. Such judgments are always subject to revision, and in fact they were constantly being revised."

Walter Rodney was among the first set of Africanist scholars who advanced the fiercest argument for the endemic underdevelopment of Africa in his book, *How Europe Underdeveloped Africa*. Since the production of that book, the study of critical race theory, with regards to race, power and culture, has never been the same again in African universities. Rodney laid a strong foundation for many African scholars to be suspicious of writings by outsiders about Africa. Mr. Karamoh Kabba seemed to have had his ears to the ground next to the notes of Walter Rodney.

Fire From Timbuktu: A Dialogue With History is a short account of Africa—pre-colonial, colonial and post-colonial, with much of its contents drawn from the famous ancient city of Timbuktu, and then used to appropriate contemporary issues on the continent. In other words, Africa is what it is because of Timbuktu and her history, obliterated by European Barbarians. It is one of those books that come into existence for the simple purpose of correcting a misnomer along the line of history. I say misnomer because, the author, Karamoh Kabba, committed himself to restoring the definitional character of Timbuktu, seeking to redefine black civilization; that is, in addition to that city's reputation of great wealth and sound education. A good name, it is said, is better than riches.

While Eurocentric history acknowledged the fact that Timbuktu had immense wealth and sound education by the year 1213-1214, much of that history had the tendency to ignore the external forces that depleted the wealth and education of Timbuktu, thus casting the blame for Timbuktu and Africa's demise on inter tribal wars across the continent. Recorded account evidence that by 1500 Timbuktu had come into fame, and remained so until the arrival of the Barbarians from Europe who plundered Africa's fame and fortune by subjecting its people in bondage for over three hundred years.

In *Fire From Timbuktu*, Karamoh Kabba argues that the savagery brought upon the African people by European Barbarians was meant to destroy any evidence of integrity and civilization the latter had made in order to subject them to slavery. These European Barbarians and colonizers, Kabba noted, "were the savages who obliterated a civilization in its cradle before it made an impact on the rest of the continent dissimilar to Athens's influence on the rest of Western nations and later on the rest of the world." With this kind of thinking, Kabba treads on the footsteps of Africanists like Cheikh Anta Diop, Frantz Fanon, and Walter Rodney. These were scholars, whose ideas were initially, fiercely challenged by the Eurocentric academic establishment, for their controversial revisionist thinking, but later, after the dust of ignorance, sentiments, and biases had settled down, they were embraced for their new and compelling scholarship. The question is in place, with *Fire From Timbuktu*, has Karamoh Kabba fashioned a place for himself among these Africanist scholars?

What is indisputable is that, *Fire From Timbuktu* attempts to achieve an ambition similar to Rodney's book, at least, that one of derailing from the 'accepted narrative' of the growth of African civilization. Kabba makes the case that Africa should "put its fine scholars to work on investigative studies on how its ancestors administered themselves hitherto the advent of colonial influence." Kabba has followed his own advice, and has taken a bold step to research and investigate Eurocentric and Afrocentric scholarship to make a case for Timbucktu historically as well as metaphorically, as a place where black people were engaged in complex political arrangements and organized educational systems long before the advent of colonialism. In fact, Kabba even postulates that Quranic and Judaic education predated European Barbarians in Africa because the pre-colonial citadels of learning had established links with their counterparts in the Arabic and Asiatic worlds.

It is important to emphasize that while Kabba's work is historical in nature, yet his desire is to point out to issues of social and economic justice. In a truly Diopian sense, Africa was coerced to abandon its own route to civilization, and to embrace the European civilization; in fact, it could be said that, Africa was rather forced to contribute to the alien civilization for the benefit of Europe. At that material time, Europe itself had not quite dug its feet into its own civilization. In Europe, the process of civilizing had only just begun. Little wonder why that first mad rush to plunder the African continent was made by bearded savages long before the first European missionaries came to plead on their behalf. In reading *Fire From Timbuktu,* one can understand why Europeans held Africans in mental and physical captivity for over three hundred years, sucking from their bodies the blood of hope of tens of generations who could have built the continent of Africa with steel, science and arts!

I hope you enjoy reading Kabba's argument.

Gbanabom Hallowell, PhD
Freetown

OVERVIEW

Just as Africanist historians state that Africa had no history prior to the advent of Europeans, so was its history on discovery, slavery, and colonialism manipulated and distorted. It was meant to keep iron grips on Africa both politically and economically. Europeans are reluctant to conclude theories that would otherwise restore the integrity of what they had discounted as a dark continent. But this is contrary to J. Michael Fay's finding in his megaflyover[1] Africa odyssey: "Despite all travails, African peoples produce magnificent art, graceful cultures, terrific music, great works of the mind, and astonishing acts of political and moral courage. Imperialist rhetoric once branded it the 'dark continent,' but that was blind and stupid, not just wrong."[2]

We also learned that in the global wars of conquest, sailing was an integral part of the lives of Africans in pursuance of territories. Great kingdoms existed in all Africa. Some historians' purport; the use of sophisticated tools had begun in Africa way before exposure to the outside world:

It has also been suggested that iron smelting may have started in Africa itself, without any outside influences, but so far none of the theories are conclusive. What we do know is that iron smelting was established in Nigeria, central Niger and southern Mali by around 500–400 BC, spreading to other parts of West Africa by 1000 AD. Iron smelting is a difficult process because the extraction of iron from rock involves a chemical process. Crushed iron ore and charcoal were placed in furnaces and lime was added. After several hours of heating, the crude iron was taken from the furnace and forged into weapons. [3]

Africans had the white man in bondage in Egypt. The foregoing fact is not just a historical one; it is also a religious fact that is well documented in both the Bible and the Koran. Africans would heed to that great religious reprimand then. By now, the pushing of dark-skinned people south had been well accomplished for the most part. Cheikh Anta Diop wrote, "What also stands out is the early arrival of the Negro on the road to civilization and the current reversal of the situation."[4] And Leo Africanus wrote when he toured Songhai, "The inhabitants are people of a gentle and cheerful disposition, and spent a great part of the night in singing and dancing through all the streets of the city."

While this experience meant civilization for Africans, Europeans where roaming the high seas in search of ill-gotten wealth that led to the taking of slaves. That is not civilization in itself. The word barbarian, which has its origin in the West, does not refer to Africans. In ancient and medieval times, it described non-Greeks and those outside of the Roman Empire—an indication that Greco-Roman civilization had not reached the entire West. While the Greeks and Romans were busy developing concepts and theories for city-states, nation-states, and global citizenship concepts, the rest of Europe was engaged in wars of conquest and less than monarchical structures based on survival of the fittest.

Similarly, many wars of conquest marked trends in ancient and medieval Africa; but at the same time, people of Jenne-Jeno and Timbuktu in Mali were busy with scholastic undertakings, such as philosophy, theology, cosmology, and city-states building ideals at the Congressional and Sankore Mosques [University of Timbuktu]. It will save us much controversy not to turn to Egypt for evidence of in-growing civilization in ancient Africa.

But before we look elsewhere for evidence, it is worth noting that Egyptian civilization could have originated from the West if the West had influenced its civilization. Much evidence suggests otherwise that Egypt is the cradle of civilization. "But in almost all the arts of life, it was the blacks who were the more advanced." The preceding sentence is an account by well-renowned historians J. D. Fage and William Tordoff of foreign infiltrations into the Western Sudan in their book A History of Africa.

It is therefore needless to delve into Egyptology, for it is well documented in many reference books. About the Western Sudan, Howard W. French writes, "Across the centuries, the Dogon[5] had developed an extraordinarily sophisticated cosmology, one replete with detailed and precise observations of the heavens, and a particular focus on Sirius, which at 8.6 light-years away is the brightest star in the sky." It appears that similar city-states political and scientific conceptual discourse among ancient Greek philosophers such as Plato and others were underway among scholars in ancient Ghana, Mali, and Songhai's Jenne-Jeno and Timbuktu. Politics and socioeconomics ideals of ancient Africa could be traced to Sultan Kunburu's assembly of scholars in Jenne in Al-Sadi's writing:

They totalled 4,200, and he made a profession of Islam before them, and told them to call upon God Most High to grant the city three things: Firstly, that anyone who fled there from his homeland in poverty and distress should have this translated by God into luxury and ease, so that he may forget his homeland; secondly, that more strangers than local folk should settle there; and thirdly, that those who came to trade there should lose patient and grow weary over selling their goods, and so dispose of them cheaply, allowing the people of Jenne to make profit.

The first part of his profession ascertained tolerance for the freedom of rights of refugees and economic travellers, the second part was an open mindedness for integration, and the third part was a strong desire and will for economic prosperity in Jenne.

But a studious close follow-up characterized the Greco-Roman philosophy unlike the destructive fate that was bestowed upon that of Jenne-Jeno's by external forces. Al-Sadi writes, "Timbuktu has been sacked three times: the first time it was at the hand of the sultan of Mossi; the second at the hand of Sunni Ali and the third at the hand of Pasha Mahmud b. Zargun . . ."

It is worth visiting Elias N. Saad's dissertation for the origin of architecture in ancient Ghana. There was a strenuous attempt by him to rectify that Al-sadi did not mean Arab al-Maghreb when he said, "The techniques of town-building came from nowhere but al-Maghreb."

Traditions which attribute the introduction of architecture from Jenne to Timbuktu would seem to point, once more, to the early influence of Dia. According to Tarikh al-Fattash, Askia Muhammad recruited fully five hundred masons from Zagha when he conquered the town. Most of these were employed in the building of Gao, the Songhai capital, while the rest built up the town of Tindirma, the capital of the eastern provinces. Al-sa'di in the 17th century seems to have been aware of these traditions and the possibility that Timbuktu partly inherited its Islamic legacy from the south. For reasons which are beyond us, he rejected these traditions quite vehemently. He neither mentioned Tadmekka nor Dia but burdened us with the assertion that civilization came to Timbuktu strictly from further west.[6]

By al-Maghreb, Al-sa'di may have meant Morocco, or the Arab, but the context of his statement suggests that he was referring to the Sahelo-sudanic west.

Everything remaining equal, there is much evidence to purport that a parallel concept to the Greco-Judeo-Christian Western civilization ideal such as the Timbuk-Traditionalist-Islamic-African civilization ideal could have outcome the religious, social, and political development in Africa. This could even be broadened further that Jenne and Timbuktu's seats of African scholarship and philosophy could have been a perfect emergence, incorporating many spiritualties and philosophies along with its exposure to Judaism, which was seeping in through the horn of Africa and Christianity afterward through the West, the East, and South Africa. Of course, Islam had been well entrenched into the African culture from North Africa or the Sahelo-sudanic West. Thus, a universal civilization well inclusive of religions, social values, and political philosophies could have become the Timbuk-Traditionalist-Islamic-Judeo-Christian African civilization.

If Africa must follow the imperial path set henceforth, its children must go back to classics upon which others built fine polities. Alternatively, Africa has the option to put its fine scholars to work on investigative studies on how its ancestors administered themselves hitherto the advent of colonial influence. History has it that the African was ruled by a Mansa (president), Mondyo and Koi (lower and upper houses of legislation), Farma (nu) (state governor(s)) and Jurists (chief justice) in Timbuktu. It was not plagued with barbarism or wars of conquest alone. Every civilization was—colonialism was not a peaceful act in the first place. It was a barbaric and inhuman act yet operated in unique ways to rule conquered subjects. Africa has the choice not to walk the barbaric path. For leadership is a long walk alongside wisdom and imprudence on a path that leads to a vast plain of innovative horizon for the present and the future.

Many, especially Africanist historians, would argue Africa was full of "savages" to have accomplished such degree of political sophistication. I am more likely to suggest that slavers and colonizers were the savages who obliterated a civilization in its cradle before it made an impact on the rest of the continent dissimilar to Athens's influence on the rest of Western nations and later on the rest of the world.

It seems that Western influence successfully stopped a developing political civilization in it track, but not its economic system and the way of life of its people. Greek philosophers did not envision monarchy, for monarchy was the order of the day in the world. Human beings lived in park of societies ruled by the strongest who instilled fear in the rest of their populations and groomed their offspring similarly to adapt themselves to carrying the kingship. Ancient philosophers acknowledged this form of political system first upon which they built better and modern political concepts and theories afterward.

For human beings or, in fact, any other animal, kingship was a no-brainer—for it just happened innately—for man is a beast without law and order, and kingship came to him instinctively as a fulfilment of his quest to control the weak in his society. A great political thinker, Cicero, in his The Republic and The Law, argued, "[I consider] the best constitution for a State to be that which is a balanced combination of the three-forms mentioned, kingship, aristocracy, and democracy, and does not irritate by punishment a rude and savage heart . . ."

To build a civilized society, it follows that a ruler must be singled out of the bunch and must be feared. There must be a selected or elected group of people who must help the leader to rule the masses, and the ruler or the masses must be the one or the ones to choose or elect these leaders in his or their own interest. Thus, a state ruled by kinship is even less dangerous than one ruled by a mob of people. And thus, Cicero and other political thinkers noted that to achieve a close-to-a-perfect democracy, a nation state must lean toward the triad system of rule. Once a good democracy is formed, should it matter then if the economic system is communism, socialism, or capitalism?

Africa's political system seemed was on a similar triad tracks combination of monarchy, aristocracy, and democracy, but on a unique economic platform, which was without these three—communism, socialism, or capitalism. I strongly believe that Africa's was "African communalism," a unique system to only Africa in modern political sense and one that complemented the African way of life both culturally and traditionally. But the advent of Western explorers, slave masters, colonialists, and cold war warriors destroyed a continent along with its civilization and call its peoples savages.

A caravan of slaves across the Sahara or a boatload of slaves across the Atlantic remains the gravest crimes against humanity. Ironically, it went on for centuries in peaceful times. A judge may set a defendant free or reduce his/her penalty based on a guilty plea of insanity driven by a provocative action. Atrocities of wars are caused mostly under such states of insanity when emotions flare up into anger where the issue of right or wrong become secondary. But even under such conditions, there are rules, which when broken surmount to war crimes. Slavery on the other hand was a war of attrition against Africans without rules, which was waged and sustained peacefully over a long period.

The slave master premeditated his trip to its minute details, said the Lord's Prayer and asked the Lord for blessing and guidance, bid his family good-bye before he set out on a journey meant to provide living for his own little children with the blood of little African children. But he has now adopted the devil's-advocate approach in a fruitless effort to justify this inhuman treatment or minimize its on-going rubber-stamped scorn on Africans with irresponsible arguments such as "slavery existed in Africa among Africans," and that "it was the order of the day then" instead of a straightforward meaningful apology and reparation. But I do not need to look any further beyond the cradle of Western civilization to refute the former and dismiss the latter arguments.

In the Politics, Aristotle argued, "Leaving out of consideration those who have been made citizens, or who have obtained the name of citizen in any other way accidental manner, we may say, first that citizen is not a citizen because he lives in a certain place, for resident aliens and slaves share in the place . . ." In the building up of civilization in ancient Mali, slavery was a component of an ideal. Thus, slaves or servants of the king readily were buried in a tomb with the king when he died. There are indications that this type of slavery was being suppressed by growing religious ideals everywhere.

In The City of God, St. Augustine (AD 354–430) wrote, "God has created man. For 'let them,' He says, 'have dominion over the fish of the sea, and over the fowl of the air, and over every creeping thing which creepeth on the earth.' He did not intend . . . man over man, but man over the beasts." The concept of slavery was universal, thus St. Augustine's great reprimand of (AD 354–430), but was not however practiced across continental boundaries as the trans-Sahara and trans-Atlantic slave trades. Regardless of who, where, and how slavery

13

was carried out, it was in contravention of such Christian and Islamic ideals that the slave master set out to Africa to capture slaves.

Frankly, there is no doubt the slave masters moved their most precious commodity, Africans, of these commercial enterprise across borders thousands of miles. Interestingly, the presence of Africans in the Arab world and the West clearly shows moderation by the former and avarice by the latter. Evidence of trans-Sahara trade is not a questionable fact, but the minimal presence of Africans across the Sahara, the Middle East, and Asia compared to the large numbers in the West at the downfall of slavery is self-evidence of the latter's greed in carrying out the trans-Atlantic slave trade, not an apology for the trans-Saharan slave trade. It is safe to believe that the first was in moderation, and the latter was a blatant disregard for a race compounded by greed.

Arab slave traders also engaged Africans intellectually and scholastically. Evidently, they contributed a great deal to the ancient history of Africa unlike Europeans who claimed Africa had no history before their so-called discovery. Many accounts of medieval and ancient African history were mostly documented by Arab scholars. Besides their religious overtones, they had paid great attention to the viewpoint of Africans versus their own point of view in many other ways.

We would need to broaden this argument further to understand Europeans' greed in carrying out the trans-Atlantic slave trade. Except genocide had been committed against Africans in the Arab nations for which there has been no evidence so far following the abolition of slavery. On the other hand, removing Africans from mainland America to its islands and repatriation to Liberia and Sierra Leone were attempted crimes of genocide perpetrated by Europeans. There was every indication that they expected them to perish. Otherwise, they would not have waited only to see Africans flourish before they returned once more to colonize them.

But was not the same European who had just reprimanded himself that slavery was bad, now back in Africa embarking on a different form of offshore slavery, away from the pressures of human rights activists to give up the bad habit and acknowledge its inhuman nature? Or were they just relying on the fact that "oh . . . well, slavery could be better carried on the continent of Africa itself" to reduce the spectre of Africans becoming predominant in their midst as well?

It is safe to believe that without institutionalized racism of the past (slavery, colonialism, imperialism, segregation, and apartheid), the world could have been more integrated by now. Human beings have that special affection and curiosity toward strangers and for strange things. As human beings, we are prone to have affection for most things new. It was probably that special affection and curiosity that worked in favour of Europeans to overcome Africans. Everything, up to the present geopolitical and socioeconomic unfairness toward Africa, has to do with institutional racism. Europe had already attained its big capitalist status, the production of everything in excess. Unlike Europe, the people of Africa were quite happy with their African communalist societies. All Africa needs is a revisit with African communalism to set a path that has been less travelled by others with a horizon for a free-market economy that is focused on not the individual or state ownership as in capitalism or communism, but the family as the smallest unit of its society.

The first reaction of these early wanderers at sea turned heisters to Africans when they stumbled upon the land and its people was fascination. It was probably with great pride that the Europeans discovered another animal of his own species that could talk, walk, and conduct business like him. It seems the whole business of slavery came about by accident when the Europeans discovered the enormous strength and prowess of Africans to work and conduct business more than they did. And Africans, who were equally fascinated by the presence of their stranger, were bent on satisfying them by trying to understand them. Communication barrier must have contributed to the misunderstanding that Africans are less inclined to learn and think.

But how could they have demonstrated such energy and skill to work if they had no knowledge of science to feed themselves and acquire the ability to work? This simply means that Europeans encountered well-nourished and ready-to-work Africans with superior thinking capacity. There has not been any report of famine or starvation in Africa before the advent of Europeans. Africans were busy tilling their land, improving their husbandry techniques and developing their hunting skills and making new version of bow and arrow, improving its range, accuracy, and handling. Plenty of food is based on very good understanding of agricultural science. Now Africa has been exposed to hunger and subsequently diseases following centuries of slaving, colonizing, and plundering. An African American missionary, William Sheppard, wrote of Kuba people of the Congo he lived among in the late nineteenth century:

These great stalwart men and women, who have from time immemorial been free, cultivating large farms of Indian corn, peas, tobacco, potatoes, trapping elephants for their ivory tusks and leopards for their skins, who have always had their own king and a government not to be despised, officers of the law established in every town of the kingdom, these magnificent people, perhaps about 400,000 in number, have entered a new chapter in the history of tribe. Only a few years ago, travellers through here this country found them living in large homes, having from one to four rooms in each house, loving and living happily with their wives and children, one of the most prosperous and intelligent of all the African tribes . . .

But within these last three years how changed they are! Their farms are growing up in weeds and jungle, their king is practically a slave, their houses now are mostly one half-built single rooms and are much neglected. The streets of their towns are not clean and well-swept as they once were. Even their children cry for bread.

Why this change? You have it in a few words. There are armed sentries of chartered trading companies who force the men and women to spend most of their days and nights in the forests making rubber, and the price they receive is so meager that they cannot live upon it. In the majority of villages these people have not time to listen to the gospel story, or give an answer concerning their soul's salvation.[7]

Why this change? I have it in two words—Western civilization. General Erskine, a British military commander in colonial Kenya in 1953 once described Kenya as "a sunny land for shady people." It was indeed the situation in most of colonial Africa, and frankly, Africans learned quite a lot from those shady settlers of General Erskine's assessment. King Leopold II was at the head of the queue of criticisms against colonial brutality in Africa only because his operations in his Congo Free State appeared to be a one-man's Western capitalist cloak for plunder. In fact, there were hardly criticisms in other colonial territories where Europeans were committing crimes against humanity at the same time.

Forced labour was to continue under the Belgian government without criticism many years after King Leopold II's death. While Leopold's death had not made a difference in Congo, about a quarter of a century later, the United States' Firestone was busy producing excess rubber through forced labour on its plantation in Liberia. Britain was sending Kikuyu Mau Mau rebels to the gallows in the bunch in British East Africa now called Kenya.

There are many accounts British people liked to visit the gallows for entertainment, in England, in the bunch. "After the trials, it was time to see the bodies swing. In the old British tradition, Baring's[8] Emergency Committee had discussed the beneficial impact of public executions at Githunguri[9], to show the Kikuyu the full might of British justice."[10] The culture they would bring to Kenya where they affected long tailcoats, round hats, tube bottom trousers, white shirts, and bow ties to look on when warders sent many Africans to the gallows. In fact, they set assizes that were intended to send as many Kikuyu to the gallows as they could with speed and efficiency.

They built gallows beside these courthouses at a distance the prisoner could see them from the courtrooms. The Mau Mau rebellion against white anachronistic rule in Kenya between 1952 and 1960 would end up claiming only thirty-two European lives that sharply contrasted with 1819 African civilians Mau Mau assassinated. Kenya was a perfect example of European divide and conquer that had Africans spending all their energy killing each other for European settlers and colonizers.

In South Africa, the Boers were busy constricting the neck of Africans as if it were a game in preparedness for apartheid. The Germans were simply ruthless with their subjects. Europeans were on a rampage, committing atrocities everywhere in Africa, while human rights organizations had King Leopold II in the limelight. It was no-brainer that Western nations were jealous of one of their own. While human rights organizations portrayed King Leopold as the lone devil in Africa, read what David Anderson wrote about life for Africans in colonial Kenya:

Among white settlers there was always a tendency to take the law into their own hands. In 1907 a crowd of settlers flogged three Africans 'rickshaw boys' on the lawn outside the Nairobi courthouse of their alleged insolence towards two European women passengers. If this was an exceptional case with a political message for a colonial state then seen to be too sympathetic to African interest, on the remote farms distant from the magistrate court, rough justice was the rule. Settlers punished their labourers and domestic staff with the kiboko, a whip made of rhinoceros hide. Floggings on the farms were part and parcel of the African worker experience. By the early 1920s, the deaths of several African servants from beatings at hands of Europeans masters earned Kenya's white settlers an unenviable reputation for brutality. [11]

But there is an end to everything. And I am proud to see that Africans won all these several wars against them. The only way to understand it is to study the intention of Europeans and their successes in other places, not by the atrocities they committed against Africans. And looking at Australia and the Americas would serve this purpose well. In both continents, the natives lost the battle against Europeans completely, and they are close to being wiped out. The native peoples of these two continents are the true endangered spices of the world today, not the zoo animals.

Europeans' intention was to take over the entire continent of Africa as they did in Australia and the Americas. This was carried out in the most brutal way. Europeans wanted the whole world for themselves. Now, one can hardly find natives on the streets of Australia and the Americas. Unlike Africa, independence has never been a dream for the native peoples of these two continents, nonetheless a reality. There is no need for us to discuss any further Africans' resilience to Europeans' oppression.

In South Africa, where Europeans almost succeeded, we saw evidence of Africans' self-determination when they sprung back. And there is no doubt Australia and the Americas tell the history Europeans failed to write in Africa. The faces of these lands are predominantly European. Now the analogy can be found everywhere among the ordinary citizens in any of these Western nations.

For example, in the United States of America, they could not do without provoking the simple animals reared for food in pursuance of the accumulation of wealth. The IHOP restaurant chain has on its all-day American breakfast menu, pigs in a blanket. It is described as having four savoury pork sausage links tucked into four tasty buttermilk pancakes.

It has come now a time when Africans must change that phrase "sunny land for shady people" to a "sunny land for transparent people." Johnnie Cochran[12], an African warrior, may his soul rest in peace—there is something Africans must learn from his greatest court legacy: "If it doesn't fit, you must acquit." The way to achieve a "sunny land for transparent people" is to shed the political and economic ideologies that turned Africa into a "sunny land for shady people" first. Apparently, they do not fit, and Africa must acquit.

19

CHAPTER ONE

'Discovery' and Slavery

In the first half of the fifteenth century, Pedro da Cintra, a Portuguese sailor, stumbled upon a beautiful West African coastline which was inhabited by the Krim, Baga, Kissi, Gola, and Nalou with the Limba people in the interior. In one account, he alluded to thunderstorms as roaring of lions in the peninsular mountain ranges along the coast of present-day Freetown and declared in Portuguese, "Serra Lyoa," meaning "Lion Mountains." In another account, history has it that he referred to the shape of the coastal mountain ranges which look like a crouching lion as Lion Mountain. Nevertheless, historians propped up him and other explorers like him in quixotic adjectives such as "discoverers." It is not surprising that in Sierra Leone, a 21st century advertisement of the main public TV broadcaster (SLBC) romanticises "Pedro da Cintra as a young Portuguese explorer who discovered Sierra Leone".

Until one reads about the atrocities one of the most acclaimed so-called explorers, Sir Henry Morton Stanley, committed in Africa, these accounts remain reinforcements of Europeans' presumptuous superior perception. Yet these are the biased historical accounts African children read in classrooms on the continent.

The distortion of the names of great nations in Africa with the advent of Europeans continued for centuries to suit the needs of people who posed as good faith traders and evangelists in the beginning before they started taking slaves. In Sierra Leone, the British came later and changed the Portuguese name Sera Lyoa to Serra Leoa, then altered it to

"Sierra Leona," further yet "Sierra Leone Company" when it became a crown colony on the 1st of January, 1808, and finally Sierra Leone before Independence. They [British] named the coastal area of Sierra Leone we now know as Freetown, the Province of Freedom, when they settled freed slaves on it on the 14th of May 1787.

The freed slaves had been forcefully removed from the interior of these same coastlines in Africa, used and tortured, had their names changed, were robbed off cultures and traditions, refused, brought back and settled on the same land they were stolen from, now called a "Province of Freedom."

Sir John Hawkins, the first 'explorer' had landed in Sierra Leone in 1562. During his third visit between 1567 and 1568, he took part in conflicts between two Mane kings "seized and took away 250 slaves. It means that the freed people did not become settlers by choice alone. They were no more desirable among Europeans following the abolition of centuries of slavery. Europeans had found out also that slavery was better yet on the continent of Africa. Away from the mounting pressure of antislavery activists, where the land, the natural resources, and the labour were in abundant supply, new forms of slavery disguised in colonialism were reintroduce.

No wonder then the British had called a whole country Sierra Leone Company. It all started as an enterprise for economic gain for them, which would become the bedrock for European heisting in the region for centuries thereafter.

A termite colony is a better analogy for slavery: In slavery, Mr. Hawkins moved up the social rank, for hard work, over and beyond. He was knighted for showing huge profits in the business of stealing people from Sierra Leone. He became a highly placed economic soldier of the British Empire, a great asset to the Crown's increased economic benefit from slavery in inverse proportion to a decrease in Africa's wealth of human resources and economic development.

This pattern of seizing people in Africa, first by Arabs [trans-Sahara slave trade] and later by Europeans [transatlantic slave trade] extended way beyond West Africa coastlines. In the European encounter with Africa, they took pleasure in naming almost every institution of learning in Africa after European royalties. They named all the beautiful natural lacustrine sceneries of East and Central Africa and the riverine settlements of West Africa after European royalties and 'explorers'. Merely, it was consistent with colonialists' over-presumptuous omniscience, which was no different from the Arabs before them.

The disregard for cultures and traditions in Africa took away more than the taking of people. It derailed the consideration of observable cultures and traditions. It nurtured inferiority complex in many Africans. It served as the root of European racism. And it entrenched stoicism in Europeans from admitting sooner that slavery was wrong.

And following flag decolonization of Africa the *Guardian* newspaper reported that historians signed a petition to repeal a French law that requires history-teaching stress on only positive aspects of slavery and colonialism. The report reads in part: "More than 1000 historians, writers, and intellectuals have signed a petition demanding the repeal of a new law requiring school history teachers to stress the 'positive aspects' of French colonialism. The report, quoting one of the petitioners, states, "'In retaining only the positive aspects of colonialism this law imposes an official lie on massacres that at times went as far as genocide on the slave trade, and on the racism that France has inherited.'"[1]

This work is a commitment to such moral position to revise the history of Africa and to urge further investigative study into how Africans ruled great kingdoms in ancient times and adapt it to present times if Africa must complete what Walter Rodney began when he wrote, "A radical break with the international capitalist system."[2] It is a call to the exigency not only to break with international capitalist system, but also with all systems that are insensitive and inconsiderate of African cultures and traditions as well as religions, values and way of life all at once.

Africa is the second largest continent in the world, the richest in both natural and human resources with 20 percent of the world's total land mass and 14 percent of the world's total population (nine hundred million).[3] It must have had unique cultures, traditional and religious observations and practices as well as political and economic systems before foreign derailment.

CHAPTER TWO

Timbuktu

The settlement of Timbuktu belongs accordingly to two main phases, which probably overlapped with each other. The first brought settlers from the northeast and south who almost certainly included scholars, both Tuareg and Soninke, from Tadmekka and Dia respectively. North African settlers long-established in these areas probably also arrived at an earlier date. But the wealthiest and most influential settlers, especially Sanhaja Berbers and North Africans from Ghadamis, arrived in the second phase which witnessed the virtual transplantation of the entire mercantile community of Walata. These were ultimately joined by Wangara merchants and scholars from the heartlands of Mali to the south and southeast, while Songhai and Fulanis [sic] may have grown in number and influence throughout the medieval period.

The ethnic diversity of the settlers naturally exerted a divisive effect, as Horace Miner has suggested, particularly since each group tended to retain its contacts and alliances with its original home. Thus, after the decline of Mali, Tuareg scholars, invariably allied to the Magsharen, enjoyed an ascendant position in the city. Later, when the Songhai Sunni Ali rose against the Tuaregs, many scholars fled back to Walata.[1]

"These were ultimately joined by Wangara merchants and scholars from the heartlands of Mali to the south . . ." Great ancestors of 19th century Mandingo immigrants into Sierra Leone must have come from Kabara to the south from the Kabari clan, which now carries several distorted forms:

24

Kaba, Kabba, Khaba, and Kabbah to name a few. Kabara was a river province of the Songhai. My last name is indicative of my ancestral origin from the Mande-speaking people of Kabara if not descendants of the founding clan there.

As distinguished scholars at the University of Timbuktu, the Kabari clan's men worked in traditionalism, Islam, and science and won many scholarly acclamations. At least that is what my grandfather meant when he said the following words: "Among my great-great-grandfathers were ulamas, big scholars, alphas; karamohs, scholars or teachers; mu'adhdhin, teachers; mujaddid, imams; mujtahid, higher scholars; philosophers; and walis, saints." They had blended ancient Timbuk-Traditionalism with Islam so well the outcome was a unique product we shall now call the "Timbuk-Traditionalist-Islamic African civilization." With further early exposures to Judaism and Christianity, this concept was bound to have become "Timbuk-Traditionalist-Islamic-Judeo-Christian African civilization."

They may have not named the ideal, but it would seem the Arabs revered the concept. Now we could make sense of the Sudanese proverb, "Salt comes from the north, gold from the south, and silver from the country of the white men, but the word of God and the treasures of wisdom are only to be found in Timbuctoo."[2] No wonder if they had sent them out farther south to spread Islam. Ellias N. Saad gives recount of the Kabari clan rise to scholarship in Timbuktu as follows:

The last years of Malian regime are better documented than earlier times and they illustrate the extent that power was shared within the city. For one thing, it seems that a substantial Malinke community had in the meantime settled in Timbuktu, which came to be distinguished in its commercial and scholarly pursuits from the Malian garrison itself. The governor who held the title of Timbuktu Koy (King of Timbuktu) was a Sanhaja Berber, originally from

Shinjit named Muhammad Nad. He seemingly did not have full command of the garrison but managed nonetheless to dispose of an armed following of his own. Even the institution of the judgeship which might have helped centralize the administration was now fragmented. For the sources confront us with three individuals each of whom is given the title of qadi.

The first is Muhammad Muaddab al-kabari, a scholar of high stature, whose descent and age became somewhat confused in the memory of the later traditionalists. He is described as a contemporary of Abd al-Rahman al-Tamimi, who flourished from 1325 onwards, and at the same time he is vaguely assigned to the 9th century A.H. Judging from his relations with a few scholars whose chronology or genealogy is known, he acted as qadi towards the very end of the Malian presence and lived for some time thereafter teaching some of the most prominent scholars of the succeeding generation. His judicial functions were probably centred on the Soninke element in the population of which he was apparently a member.[3]

The foregoing is conceptualization blended with knowledge of oral tradition backed by research and recounts. However, on the other hand, the persecution concept is further compelled by John Hunwick's translation of Al-SaᶜdꞮ's Taᴼrīk al-sūdān in his book, Timbuktu and the Songhai Empire: Down to 1613 and other Contemporary Documents (Islamic History and Civilization)

"Sunni Ali anticipated the Timbuktu scholars' opposition to his rule and moved against them swiftly when he conquered the city in 1468. Many fled to Walata, and many of those who remained behind lost their lives" when he collaborated with the Moroccan invaders following the conquest of the Songhai. Some ancestors of the 19th century Madingo people of Sierra Leone, many generations ago, must have been students of Modibo Muhammad al-Kabari[4] or his direct descendants whose, according to Al-Saᶜdī's Taᴼrīk al-sūdān, native town was Kabara in the west of Jenne.

Actually, in Mandinka or Soninke tribes, Kabari means a "dweller of Kabara," and Kabara means "at the town of Kaba." "Kabara had produced many scholars who had taken up residence in Timbuktu," Al-Saᶜdī's Taᴼrīk al-sūdān wrote. From Walata, in a group of Kabari clan scholars, they must have travelled south around Songhai and sailed on the river Niger southward where they could have sailed the Senegal River, deep South, and settled in Bundu over hundreds of years of migrations, settlements, and resettlements similar to the earlier migration of the Kono people.

Many must have gone their separate ways along the way; the presence of Madingo people especially the Kabari or Kaba clan offspring all around the Senegal region, Mali, Guinea, and Sierra Leone is further evidence of the migrations and separations.

The presence of the Kaba clan in Egypt does not only support the Walata northbound flight, but also jolts ones curiosity. Cheikh Anta Diop's ethnological study, The African Origin of Civilization, turned out much evidence among many West African clans the presence of the Kaba clan in Egypt and Senegal. We know about two major events that could have made it possible. One is the pushing of dark-skin people south by present day light-skin northerners. Two is the flight of the Timbuktu scholars northward Walata, from where they probably separated, those that came southward and those that could have continued northward to Egypt.

But my grandfather lived enough longer to learn from previous generations how his forebears came to Senegal, which he passed on to me in the story of his journey from Bundu to Sierra Leone, which took place in the last quarter of the nineteenth century.

My grandfather was very passionate about Islamic scholarship. Up to now, we have relatives in Bundu. Before my grandfather died in 1988, he had sent some of my brothers to Senegal to be schooled as Islamic scholars to uphold the tradition of Koranic scholarship of his forebears. They returned to Peyima for his burial, but we quickly saw that they could not live among us and subsequently went back to Bundu. Ours had been influenced so much by the Kono tradition and culture and theirs by Islam that they look at everything we do as *harram*.[5]

My family's cultural and traditional structure is a two-way street. My grandfather himself had become a big influence on the Kono community of Peyima; many Peyima residents became Islamic converts. He accomplished great things, including the recognition of becoming the first miner of diamonds in Peyima. He built a big compound in Peyima, a mosque that was designed similar to that of Jenne-Jeno's, but far less sophisticated and smaller, a madrassa where many children of Kono Islamic converts were taught Koranic studies and several pilgrimages to Mecca in a harem.

On his second trip to Mecca, he travelled with and was responsible for twelve pilgrims. My grandmothers were all hajjas.[6] He was a strong believer in Islam, and he prayed fervently and fasted in the month of Ramadan in fulfilment of the five pillars of Islam, a tradition that he passed on to my father. This is, in fact, evidence that supports the notion my ancestors, many generations ago, had probably left Kabara to propagate Islam and kept on going on generations after generations.

But he told intriguing stories about his journey. Most interesting is the oral tradition about his forebears he passed down to us. His longevity is somewhat evidence of the active life he had lived. He was so old that we (grandchildren and great-grandchildren) took turns in his geriatric care. We relieved our siblings, who did not go to school[7], of this responsibility when we went to Peyima on vacation. We bathed, dressed, and fed him. Up to his death, his memory was sharp even though he had lost to arthritis the ability to walk. He could recognize all of us and called us by our names.

As if oral tradition was the reward he gave for taking care of him, he passed down to us these intriguing stories of his life. Amazingly, he always knew where he had stopped the last time it was my turn to take care of him from where he would continue. If I did not like taking care of him, his stories were fascinating, and he knew that I had much interest in his narratives.

He was a man of enormous stature in his days with very prominent and imposing features. One day, while we were moving him from his bed to his commode, I slipped and nearly dropped him. But he was shaken so badly it scared the hell out of him. His bones were so obvious as though they will prick out of his frail skin. The look on his face only reminded me of Sir H. Rider Haggard's "Gaggle Pass through the Door" description in King Solomon's Mines. He refused to narrate his story and called me a name. But when he did, the next day, I would always be the only one left in the room, and I enjoyed every word he said. He knew the Koran in and out to the point he could recite the verses by heart.

It seems his great grandparents had been travelling with their herds from generation to generation from Mali/Songhai. They were well-read Islamic scholars. I saw my own great-grandfather. I was sensible enough to remember what he told me about the family. He told me that his own great-grandfather was chosen by the tibabukeh (white man)[8] to spread Islam south among the kafir— pagans. "Even though I did not fight any of these battles myself, my grandfather fought many wars alongside his own father about which he talked to me," he explained. "Theirs," he continued, "was actually fighting the actual head of Satan, the devil. Not only was it difficult to convert these people of the South to Islam." He would stress, "They waged wars on them no sooner they condemned their fetish methods of doing things."

Much of traditionalism that had been lost to Islam among the Mandingo people could be seen observed by the Kono people.

CHAPTER THREE

The Kono People

There are several accounts to the history of the Kono people, but the most popular is that the Kono people are offspring of wearied Mandingo warriors who their fellow, more competent Mandingo warriors left about two hundred miles inland off the coast of present-day Sierra Leone to wait, but did not return for. It would seem they had been conquered and marginalized by stronger Mande-speaking group of warriors in ancient Ghana. This would be from where they would have headed farther south with empty scabbards and naked swords in a pursuit of freedom and better living conditions way before the influence of Islam in the Western Sudan.

Not much has been written about the Kono people. Apparently, they are not part of the grand Arab scholarly accounts of the people of the Western Sudan. That further explains they had migrated or fled the region before Arab infiltration or right around that time. Thus, among the Kono people is the untouched and unhampered Timbuk-Traditionalism that is characterized by matriarchal powers and secret societies. Blessed is Robert T. Parsons whose authoritative religious study of the Kono people gives us some insight of them and their culture. A work Robert would dedicate to the Kono people with these words, "To the Kono people among whom God has left himself without a witness." The following are the legends he wrote,

The Kono people probably entered their present home from a section of hilly country to the east of Sierra Leone in

Guinea. This fact seemingly corroborated by the Kono legends. The people speak of their former home as "Kono-su-ko" (under- the Kono-root) taken from Kono-su the name of a hill in Guinea about fifty miles northwest of Konoland. The people who now live about this hill speak a language said to be like the Kono language, but the people are called the Lelli people. The Lelli people are said to be almost surrounded today by the Kissi and Koranko groups. The Kono people probably entered Konoland three centuries ago with their cows, sheep, and goats. Sometime later, they were attacked by the Mendis and sought refuge among the Korankoes [*sic*] to the north for about ten years. The departure of the Mendis [*sic*] to their own territory in this interim permitted the Konos [*sic*] to up their own land.

The second legend that points to their origins is the one giving their relation to the Vai people, a group now living along the Sierra Leone-Liberia border near the coast. The legend is this: the Kono and Vai peoples were probably the same tribe when they came into this land from the northeast searching for salt, which they had heard was plentiful along the coast. But when the Kono came to their present land, with its abundance of wild game and much good farming land, they decided to stay and occupy it. So they said to the Vai people, "We will wait (makono) for you." The Vai went on to the coast where they found the salt they had longed for, leaving the Kono people still waiting for their return.

When the Kono people occupied their present land, they found small steatite or soapstone carvings, which they believe, were made by "Nyina-nu" (the spirit). Hence, they have come to look upon them as mysterious and containing some magical power. They can be seen in the court buildings where they are used as the objects upon which the people swear before testifying.[1]

We know about those who went south to become the Vai people of coastal Sierra Leone. But we know very little about those that went farther north of Sierra Leone. But it would appear the Koranko people, another voracious warrior-like Mande-speaking group, pushed them back eastward. These were probably the Kono people of one of Robert's legends, who became the southern neighbours of the Koranko people of the north of Sierra Leone. It appears that the Koranko people, who are also of the same Mandinka and Soninke origin as the Kono, must have left ancient Ghana right around or the same time. Robert's three hundred years estimation, which is now about 355 years since he did his research, makes much sense because it corresponds with the Arab invasions of Timbuktu. They, too, as if to say they had arrived at their destination at last, settled in their new home in the northern province of Sierra Leone and named it Kabala, a probable distortion of Kabara, the place of their origin in ancient Ghana, southwest of Timbuktu.

But the word *Kabala* is mostly an evidence of distortion due to centuries of migration. Robert had suggested the beginning of their migration as three hundred years ago when he wrote his book on the Kono people in 1964. This seems to support the notion they came to the Konoland, alongside the other Mande-speaking groups, who would become Koranko people and must have by now lay down their constant migration to rest about the same time. Simply because Kabala borders the Konoland may mean that all these Mande-speaking groups had been locating and relocating constantly toward the coast of West Africa, from the ancient Ghana, for at least two hundred years. This surely explains why the accent and forms of the Mandinka language had been changing constantly, thereby resulting into these several subgroups as Kono, Vai, Koranko, and Lelli.

The *Historical Dictionary of Sierra Leone* states about the Kono people, "Kono tradition asserts that the Kono were once a powerful people in present-day Guinea or Mali or both."[2] This tempts to be consistent with the notion of hundreds of years of their constant migration, settlement, and resettlement. The same work states about the Koranko people, "A branch of the Madinka tribe, the Koranko, immigrated into Sierra Leone from Guinea, probably at the time of the Mane invasions, possibly in the last waves of the invasion."[3]

We know very little of why they must have split along the way and where or when. Some historians were able to trace Kono and Koranko peoples at separate places in the Guinea. Just as the same Mande-speaking group became Kono and Vai in Guinea, it is highly suspicious that they had become Kono and Koranko somewhere along the way over these hundreds of years. With my patriarchal Mandingo and matriarchal Kono backgrounds, I certainly understand or speak all these dialects of the Mandingo language variations.

Although Robert's work, unlike many Africanists historians, is sympathetic of his subjects, apparently, some facts were lost in translation or misunderstood. Now the stone carvings, which Robert described in his work as having pierced noses, are likely indicative of earlier Soninke and Mandinka cultural presence in the area. When the European drew a European Jesus, all he had seen around him was a white man. Thus, the Soninke and Mandinka cultures, which are big on ear, nose, and lip piercing, could have certainly used nose piercing as an element of their works of art.

The Kono word *Nyina* means "devil" instead of "spirit" according to Robert. The traditionalist Kono people could not have used a devil as a symbol of spirituality. But the misunderstanding is apparent in Robert's work; he rightfully placed the carvings as a symbol of spirituality, but wrongly called them devils. The traditionalist Kono people used these carvings, which were perceived mysteries to them as medium between them and *Yatah* (God). But the carvings were nothing but Soninke or Mandinka works of art that were lost to mystery amid constant migrating and warring over hundreds of years.

The mystery in the existence of a Supreme Being is so compelling in the traditionalist Kono culture that the Kono people refer any matter that is beyond their knowledge that which cannot be discerned by human beings to *Yatah*. But Robert confused Kono traditionalism when he called *Yatah* ancestral spirits. The Kono people, up to this present day, whether they have become Christians or Muslims have hardly given up the value they attach to ancestral spirits as a medium to *Yatah*. This fact is entirely different from the unintentional distortion of referring to *Yatah* as ancestral spirits.

Another argument is that *Yatah* is a singular noun. Plural nouns in the Kono language take the suffix "*nu*." First, a plural word for *Yatah* does not exist in the Kono language. If at all there were ancestral spirits called *Yatah*, they would have been called *Yatahnu*. But it turned out that there is no such word in the Kono language. This in itself is a clear indication that a one Supreme Being concept existed in Kono traditionalism before Western influence. Words for gods and goddesses are entirely different from the Supreme Being, *Yatah*. Second, the word for ancestral spirit is *fuyeh* and its plural is *fuyehnu*. I am afraid the Kono people would have used the word *Yatanu* if at all they meant to refer to ancestral spirits as God. And the importance of this personal anecdote to this work is an attempt to trace the unhampered Timbuk-Traditionalist culture before Islam.

Another issue with Robert's work is that the Kono people could not have been in search of salt. The history of the Kono people points to invasions of some sort at all times, it is questionable how the search for salt came into play. Salt was an abundant element of trade in Gao, the capital city of the ancient Ghana. What the Kono people had probably said was *cheh*, meaning "war." The same word is *chereh* in Mandinka. But it is obvious that the early Africanists heard *kuyeh*, which means, "salt." There is no way the Kono people could have left Gao in search of salt all the way to their present location. Even the most sympathetic Western Africanists writers and historians very often have tempted to misinterpret African peoples' traditions and cultures unintentionally or intentionally.

Nonetheless, this then heightens ones curiosity that the Kono and the Mandinka peoples must have come from the same ancestral heritage from Ghana/Mali. It is probable that the Kono must have come out of ancient Ghana before it was Mali and Songhai or about the period of its transition to Mali and Songhai.

Like most Mande-speaking groups, the Kono and Mandinka dialects are distinct only by accent and few words. But it became obvious why predominantly, the former practices traditionalism and the later practices Islam. This further heightens the suspicion that the Kono people had no or very little exposure to Islam before they left the ancient Ghana unlike the Mandingo people who had been exposed to Islamic civilization before they left the Mali/Songhai. This is evident in the obvious distinct religious beliefs between them: traditionalism versus Islam, the Kono and Mandingo peoples respectively.

According to oral tradition, it would appear that either late Mandingo settlers in Sierra Leone many generations back were Islamic scholars whom Arab scholars sent southward to propagate Islam, or had fled at an earlier period from persecution southward many years, following the Kono people's migration. "For years, they had ridiculed the Songhai as ignorant and considered their king a Muslim in name only. Sonni Ali to his revenge sacked the city and killed thousands of Islamic leaders, chasing the rest into the desert."[4] The tradition was not only supported by Al-sa'di's account, but by many other scholars who have done much research on the Ghana/Mali and Mali/Songhai in recent times.

36

CHAPTER FOUR

Slavery and Colonialism

On April 27, 1961, the duke of Kent exchanged the Union Jack for the Green White and Blue flag in Freetown, Sierra Leone, a process which had begun in 1957 in Ghana when Harold McMillan, then British prime minister, dubbed the burning desire for independence across Africa the "Wind of Change." Many countries in Africa were fighting for independence or had just had one around that time in history. And in the late fifties, sixties to the mid-seventies, the wind of change was blowing so fiercely, the entire royal family was involved with the process across Africa because the queen of England could not keep up with the busy schedule of swapping flags.

In Sierra Leone, it all began in 1787 when Britain set up the Province of Freedom on the peninsula, which became a haven for freed slaves from Britain, Jamaica, United States, and Canada. Britain was a knowledgeable empire builder with considerable experience in walking on thin threads. And Sierra Leone would escape from becoming the origin of the brutal rebel war that began in Liberia in 1989, which could have happened if the educated freed people were allowed to form a monarchy to rule the hinterland people in Sierra Leone.

That was exactly what would happen in neighbouring Liberia when the American Colonization Society founded that nation in 1822. The idea was first proposed in 1800: "Following a thwarted Virginia slave uprising that resulted in the hanging of some 35 slaves. Virginia delegates called upon President Thomas Jefferson to purchase lands 'where persons obnoxious to the laws or dangerous to the peace of society may be removed.'" [1]

The American Colonization Society thought the Province of Freedom in Sierra Leone was a novel idea. "Jefferson initially proposed a joint effort with Great Britain, which had already started a colony for former slaves in Freetown, Sierra Leone, but rising tensions that would eventually culminate with the War of 1812 stalled Jefferson's[2] proposal."[3]

This would be the plan that Francis Scott Key, Daniel Webster, and Henry Clay would awaken four years later under the American Colonization Society, which was strongly supported by James Monroe[4]. But the American Colonization Society either was short sighted or had plotted an attempted genocide against the black man. "When an outsider comes into a new ecological system, even if he is more skilled he does not necessarily function as effectively as those who have familiarized themselves with the environment over centuries; and the newcomer is likely to look more ridiculous if he is too arrogant to realize that he has something to learn from the 'natives.'" [5]

In Sierra Leone, the British oversaw the Province of Freedom through the Sierra Leone Company. Unlike the British, the United States brokered a very bad deal with the aborigines in Liberia. It was not concerned about the safety of its freed people who the American Colonization Society would dump on this piece of small land wedged between English and French colonial territories, which are present-day Sierra Leone, Guinea, and Ivory Coast.

It would seem that the American Colonization Society saw the fear of freed slaves becoming revolutionary in America was the main reason behind the resettlement plan. Adam Hochschild writes, "Like most Southern politicians of the era, he was frightened by the spectre of millions of freed slaves and their descendants harbouring threatening dreams of equality," referring to Senator John Tyler.

Indeed, the strong survival instinct and high fertility rate of the black man was surely increasing the black population at an alarming rate that spurred the need to get rid of him. Thus, this piece of land, which the United States named Liberia, became a hotbed for trouble from the outset when the American Colonization Society quickly dumped the content of its vessels and left the freed people to face a survival of the fittest. It would also seem they chose that area because of its known unfriendliness to Westerners. More or less, they did not expect the repatriated freed black slaves to survive.

Indeed, almost all the freed people from the first vessel died, including the three agents who went with them. The survivors would be evacuated to Freetown. But they brought more, now rest assured their presumption was correct. Why would they keep bringing more if the first birch barely survived? Once again, the innate survival instinct of the black man would prove itself on the land the Europeans and other Westerners had labelled the white man's grave when he thrived.

But the settlers, some of whom were highly educated before coming to Liberia, would turn on their own kind and, for one and half century, subjugated the aborigines who had kind-heartedly accepted them. The settlers carried out the subjugation of the aborigines with heavy-handed support from the United States. To make matters worse, an American company by the name of Firestone returned to Liberia and compounded subjugation by slave labour on what became the world's biggest rubber plantation. These cruel treatments victimized the aborigines for the most part for over a century. This is most articulated by Howard W. French:

This same gritty resourcefulness was at work at the International Hotel, once a majestic skyscraper that stood on the city's ground like an exclamation point, announcing the cosmopolitan pretensions of the old Americo-Liberian elite—the class of freed American slaves that had founded this country in 1847. As they settled the land, the Americo-

Liberians fondly strove to reproduce the only model they know, the plantation society of the American South. Affecting top hats and morning coats, the freedmen ruled Africa's first republic in a clannish and conservative manner, established their own curiously paternalistic brand of apartheid, systematically excluding so-called aborigines from positions of privilege and power until 1980, when a coup by an unschooled soldier and "man of the soil" from the Krahn ethnic group, Master Sergeant Samuel Kanyon Doe, brought this anachronistic little universe to a bloody end.[6]

There is a parallel between the American Colonization Society and International Society of the Congo. The former is the origin of the destabilization of West Africa and the latter, DR Congo, Uganda, Burundi, Rwanda, and Angola. Both of them were deceptive—capitalists' interest cloaked in humanitarian reason. Both used forced labour on rubber plantations. United States probably did not colonize Liberia because of the possible international criticism the action could have mustered—it would have been quite a story for a nation that had just won its independence. But it sure accomplished the same goal in Liberia as any other colonial power in Africa.

In 1930, the League of Nations report exposes forced labour practices in Liberia by Firestone Corporation. The United States' relation with Liberia was consistent with every other colonial power in post-independence Africa—capitalist imperialism.

The truth is any society whose leadership pushes it around too long and heavy-handedly becomes a time bomb. "The city is divided into rich rulers and poor subjects. In the soul of the oligarchic man, pleasure-loving but ungenerous, the desiring part prevails over the reasoning and spirited parts. The oligarchic constitution degenerates into democracy when the poor in the oligarchic state revolt. All are then set free to do as they wish—and, says Socrates in effect, to go to the devil in their own way." [7]

Inhuman treatment of the aborigines in Liberia by Americo-Liberian settlers surely created such a perfect condition that would become the destabilization force for the Economic Community of the West African States (ECOWAS) region. The rice (pusawah) price hike of 1979 is a secondary reason to the most potent political one that had set Liberia on a springboard for war. Even though the rebel war affected Liberia and Sierra Leone the most, their neighbours shared some of the burden. The media reported little skirmishes in Guinea here and there, Sierra Leone pointed fingers at Burkina Faso for staging beachheads for rebel forces and the diplomatic corps implicated Ivory Coast for sponsoring rebels against Samuel Doe. Late Félix Houphouët-Boigny, a long-time dictator in Ivory Coast loathed Samuel Doe for killing William Tolbert.[8] Nigeria and Ghana carried on their shoulders heavy financial and military burdens. Refugee crises plagued almost every country in the ECOWAS region. Tarty Teh explains:

Dr. Patrick Seyon was the water boy for the band of Americos who first coalesced as ACDL (Association for Constitutional Democracy in Liberia) which, according to Mr. Greaves, "operated on two tracks and at two levels" from Washington, D.C. Apparently Dr. Seyon was aware of only the track that led to the U.S. Capitol Hill where he was led to deliver a testimony against an elected government of President Samuel Doe. As I remember his testimony in early 1990, it was Dr. Seyon's belief –echoed later by Mr. Francis Afonso Dennis, former Liberian ambassador to Washington in the lost dispensation—which democracy was on the horizon in Liberia in 1980 when the People's Redemption Council (PRC) overthrew the 130-year-old Americo Liberian Empire. It was that apparently slow-rising democracy that was aborted by the coup that removed the last Americo president (before Charles Taylor) from office.[9]

It is probable that the United States had also used Liberia for military purposes. Liberia seemed like a beachhead for the pentagon for many years and therefore was very important to the United States. Evidently, the U.S. currency was the medium of exchange in a small country far away out of the reach of even the likes of Abraham Lincoln.[10] Whereas Washington observed this small country thousands of miles away from mainland United States had become a destabilizing ground for the U.S. dollars, it would seem that the military importance of Liberia to the United States was so compelling that the US could afford to have its currency hanging loose there, being thrown either thither by those who Washington referred to as shady business people and terrorists. And rumour has it that Washington failed to persuade late president William Tolbert to surrender the use of the U.S. dollars. And that the CIA may have been behind the Doe bloody coup to overthrow William Tolbert.

But that is all speculations; we know for sure that Liberia had gone wrong exactly hundred and sixty years ago when the first American Colonization Society's ship, the Elizabeth, left the shores of the United States in 1820. There is no doubt that the United States was also concerned with Soviet influence in Liberia under an inexperience leader as Doe 161 years later. The United States provided aid in the tune of $500 million to the Doe government between 1981 and 1985. Chester Crocker, assistant secretary of state for African affairs under then president Ronald Regan would argue, "The United States had an obligation to Liberia. It had vested intelligence and commercial interests and an infrastructure there, and cutting off aid could lead to regional destabilization and increasing Soviet and Libyan involvement."[11]

No wonder that President Reagan's secretary of state, George P. Shultz, went to Liberia to endorse the first presidential election in 1985 following the coup and expressed the following regret after meeting Doe: "Perhaps I made a wrong career choice, if it was people like that I was going to meet. Doe was unintelligible."[12] Doe had outright stolen the election in 1985.

And this pattern of supporting dictators and despots for interest is not a new phenomenon. Realpolitik has been the adopted policy by Western nations for Africa in the sphere of political ideological and economics influence. Thus, the insidious manner in which Washington settled its currency crisis in Liberia made the currency rumour compelling even without empirical evidence. Especially that Doe would change the Liberia currency from the U.S. dollars to Doe dollars, a currency which would become as worthless as a roll of Scott Tissue by the end of that year. Even seasoned researchers would be tempted for an explanation on how this unprecedented change of currency in Liberia from U.S. dollars to Doe dollars came about following that bloody coup staged by Doe in Liberia.

Nonetheless, like many other despots in Africa, Doe must protect his power base by cleansing the political atmosphere. He killed not only his supercilious political rivals, but also his comrades in the struggle to overthrow Pres. William Tolbert. The simple reason is, a man such as Gen. Thomas Quiwonkpa[13], with his known valour, all he needed was a desire to take power from Doe, and nothing could stop him from trying, and so were many of his comrades in arms in the coup plot with him to overthrow William Tolbert. This was a fair threat to his power base as far as Doe was concerned. But even without a base to eliminate his friends, now turned political enemies, doing so created a peace of mind, he needed to cling on to power like many more African leaders.

CHAPTER FIVE

Historical Wrongs and Political Miscalculations

Since foreign infiltration derailed its great kingdoms from self-rule, the continent suffered two major setbacks: slavery and colonialism. Europeans encountered, conquered, and colonized many peoples around the world. They went a step further to dehumanize Africans into mere commodity. Slavery was a double-edge-sword approach in Africa compared to the rest of the world.

Next was colonization, which was a modified form of slavery on the continent. It was not only a modified form of slavery; it was also a destruction of entire political, economic, cultural, and traditional systems. Europeans reduced great nation-states in Africa into too many small countries to render them manageable and plunderable from thousands of miles away. Unlike slavery, these small territories were owned and run by European governments far away from abolitionists' pressure.

The exigency to plunder Africa was so important to European nations there was no time to go to war over it. The actors must have cautioned themselves that the land, its human, and its natural resources were abundant. And there was no need to fight.

In Berlin, in the late nineteenth century, they affected dark suits—complete with white shirts, bow ties, and tall hats—sat across conference desks, and peacefully apportioned Africa. No African was present, but their owners, for only commodities are apportioned in that

44

manner. Before that, Europeans were all over Africa in much disorganized ways, capturing and selling slaves. They, henceforth, continued the plundering of territories that were now formally assigned to them at the Berlin Conference.

This formal apportioning of territories among European colonialists was a blow, below the belt, to human rights activists who had ended slavery in Europe and America. They became powerless because the new chief executive officers for these new enterprises across Africa were European nation-states, away from western lands.

This newly formed institutional slavery lasted until the "wind of change" that fomented in Ghana blew over Africa along with colonialists' flags. That was the second major victory against slavery that, nonetheless, blew away only the colonialists' flags. And the Europeans granted Africa economic imperialism, another version of slavery afterward.

Now Europeans further suppressed the political consciousness of African peoples to continue the plundering of the African continent in this modification of slavery and colonialism. This dangerous type of freedom became the prerequisite for the battle of Eastern and Western Europe, a sphere of ideological influence political ideologues dubbed the cold war. One of the many battlegrounds and probably the most important one was Africa.

Indeed, economic and political imperialism became the last straw that broke the already-aching camel's back. It was indeed a cold witch-hunt on the African political freedom of choice. Its spleen was way venomous than that of H. Rider Haggard's fallacious depiction of sorcery in Kukuanaland, where Twala the King's Gagool earmarked political rivals for death in his Oxford World's Classics, *King Solomon's Mines.*

The cold war sorcerers were Eastern and Western Europeans' secret agents. Their targets were three types of pre-independence African leaders: Those that leaned toward Marxist political ideology, those that leaned toward Western ideology, and those nonaligned empty demagogues, who apparently had no alternative political ideals of their own.

Western European secret agents witch hunted Marxist followers and portrayed sainthood for their allies. The reverse was true for Marxist sorcerers.

Indeed, colonial powers were determined to protect their capitalist interests and prevent international communist influence in these young nations. They knew much too well that the Soviet Union was poised for a share of the rich African market, especially its raw material. Certainly, an influence over the political system in Africa would subsequently mean greater control of its raw materials. The process was far from being normal diplomacy, but through political subversion by coercion, covert actions, yet still overt actions in some cases. This political ideological rivalry between Eastern and Western Europe over Africa added salt to injury, especially at a time when Africa was grappling with its problematic ideal of unifying its many boundaries the very colonialists had created.

Thus, it would seem Britain's consideration to include its former empire states in the Commonwealth of Nations was not out of benevolence for post-independence African nations. It seemed like a political stratagem that lured sprouting leaders in its former colonies into apprenticeship to capitalism. Indeed, African economies are heavily depended on farming and mining—production of raw material for Western industries and weapon manufacturers.

To keep it that way, African nations must remain dependent on European economies. Thus, the Commonwealth of Nations was more or less an imperialist tool: a cloak that Britain and other Western nations benefited from when they closed up large mandibles on African natural resources and based its body politic on European cultures, traditions, and values. How else do we explain that the Commonwealth of Nations, established in 1931, changed and redefined its membership to include independent nations in 1947 at the dawn of independence in Africa, but withheld major Commonwealth of Nations' rights and privileges from Africans right around the collapse of communism?

Before the infiltration of Soviet Union that facilitated glasnost under Mikhail Gorbachev, Western powers supported undemocratic regimes in Africa regardless of their autocratic or despotic dispositions for the same reason. Many of these leaders, mostly military conscripts, gained political support from the West because they were allies and were willing to prevent the spread of communism in Africa. It was a sufficient criterion for Western support: The silent war that distracted true African leadership, the silent war that derailed African nationalism, the silent war that impaired economic innovations, and the silent war that bred corruption, money grubbing, ruthlessness, and civil wars.

The birth of civil wars in Africa is connected to the cold war:

Moscow invested far greater hopes and resources in Angola, Mozambique and Ethiopia than it had done in Ghana, Guinea and Mali a decade or more earlier. It also made much more extensive use of its allies, especially Cuba and East Germany, to defend the new Marxist regimes against their opponents than it had ever done before. Castro, in particular, was a willing and at times enthusiastic ally.[1]

In Africa, one such ally, who later came on stage, was Muhammad Qaddafi of Libya. Qaddafi and Fidel Castro, both Marxism cohorts, both in denial to acknowledge the end of the cold war continued to fight on many years later, thereby fuelling civil wars in Africa and Central and South America. In a fervent refusal to concede defeat, they flamed political conflicts in other third world nations when they stood up to the victorious Western powers of the war of political sphere of influence. This is the war (cold war), at its height in the seventies, in the aftermath of the collapse of the Portuguese Empire of Angola and Mozambique, along with the pro-Western regime of the Lion of Judah, Emperor

Haile Selassie of Ethiopia to pro-communist leaders, the Tanzanian president Julius Nyerere called the "second scramble" for Africa. In effect, the KGB made its intention to undermine the Americans and British in Africa very clear. From 1976 to 1981, Soviet military aid to black Africa totalled almost four billion dollars. Because of this massive military aid to pro-communist leaders in Africa, Ethiopia levied a massive defeat on Somalia in 1978. When the two countries locked horns, the Soviets fell out with Somalia simply because Ethiopia was a better country of interest and abandoned Somalia that became a pro-Western country. Almost no Soviet success story in Africa was without Cuba every step of the way.

One good outcome of Cuba being in Africa was the part credit accorded Fidel Castro for the downfall of apartheid in South Africa. He received a red-carpet reception from Nelson Mandela in the new democratic South Africa for helping to boost the morale of the African National Congress (ANC) leadership. Indeed, it seemed though the massive jaws of South Africa's apartheid regime actually became toothless not because of the presence of Cuban troops in Angola, but more because the United States had put down communism. For many freedom fighters in Africa and the Americas who shared Marxist aspiration before them met their demise simply because of their political preference that was abhorrent to the United States.

"Lumumba's greatest affront, however, was his decision to accept substantial Soviet aid in order to attack the secessionist areas. This move brought to a climax the issue of communist influence, which had been a source of growing concern to the West and to more moderate Africans-alike."[2] Qaddafi and Fidel's efforts to hold on to leftist ideology were like a beheaded serpent still wanting to strike, even though the Soviet Union had been highly infiltrated, and was either crumbling or had crumbled.

Therefore, it seemed that the fall of communism helped the West to ease down on its support for apartheid in South

Africa. Before that, the apartheid regime had managed to gain Western support simply by accusing Mandela of communism. "Communism was suspect not only in the West but in Africa. This came as something of a revelation to me, and it was a view that I was to hear over and over during my trip."[3]

Late president Ahmed Sékou Touré of Guinea, a benevolent dictator, became an outright tyrant because KGB agents fed him with information of plot by pro-Western politicians to assassinate him. This dangerous Soviet cold war weapon changed many post-independent Africa's leaders into tyrants. Besides, Touré had an affinity for communist's one-party idealism, which he used to hold on to power in the face of fierce opposition. He suppressed cold war political rivalry through absolute power and tyranny. The Soviet Union in turn embarked on grandiose aid to Guinea onto sending snowploughs in a country it never snowed. But he, too, would meet a sudden death in 1984. Many people in Africa have speculations that Western Europe had hands in his death for tipping more to the left.

The former French and British colonies failed to live up to Khrushchev's expectations. Apart from Nkrumah, the only members of the first generation of African leaders to arouse the serious interest of the KGB were the Francophone Marxist dictators of Guinea and Mali, Ahmed Sékou Touré and Modibo Keïta. In all three cases, however, the centre's hopes were dashed. As well as creating one-party states, Nkrumah, Touré and Keïta wrecked their countries' economies, leaving Moscow wondering whether to pour good money after bad to bail them out.[4]

Adam Hochschild's account seems to suggest that CIA agents masterminded the murder of Patrice Lumumba of DR Congo because of his communist/socialist affiliation. "I heard a CIA man, who had had too much to drink, describe with satisfaction exactly how and where the newly independent country's first prime minister, Patrice Lumumba, had been killed a few months earlier."[5] But that of Andrew and Mitrokhin suggests otherwise:

On Eisenhower's instructions, the CIA had prepared a plan to poison Patrice Lumumba, the pro-Soviet prime minister of the Republic of Congo, later renamed Zaire. In the event, Lumumba was murdered in December 1960 not by the CIA but by his Congolese rival, Joseph Mobutu, who went on to become one of the most corrupt of independent Africa's kleptomaniac rulers.[6]

Stephen R. Weisman wrote in the July 21, 2002, edition of the *Washington Post* newspaper:

I have obtained classified U.S. government documents, including a chronology of covert actions approved by a National Security Council (NSC) subgroup, that reveal U.S. involvement in—and significant responsibility for—the death of Lumumba, who was mistakenly seen by the Eisenhower administration as an African Fidel Castro. The documents show that the key Congolese leaders who brought about Lumumba's downfall were players in "Project Wizard," a CIA covert action program. Hundreds of thousands of dollars and military equipment were channelled to these officials, who informed their CIA paymasters three days in advance of their plan to send Lumumba into the clutches of his worst enemies. Other new details: The U.S. authorized payments to then-President Joseph Kasavubu four days before he ousted Lumumba, furnished Army strongman Mobutu with money and arms to fight pro-Lumumba forces, helped select and finance an anti-Lumumba government, and barely three weeks after his death authorized new funds for the people who arranged Lumumba's murder.[7]

Whatever the case may have been, Mobutu's thirty-year marriage with the United States and divorce right around before his death is additional information for the reader to make a sound judgment.

Kwame Nkrumah of Ghana took refuge in Guinea following an attempted assassination on his life in a military coup d'état. His successor went on to expel all communist agents out of Ghana and severed military relations with Moscow. No one explains Nkrumah's tangle in capitalism and communism better than Christopher Andrew and Vasili Mitrokhin in their book *The World Was Going our Way: The KGB and the Battle for the Third World.*

Khrushchev's interest in Africa was much greater than Stalin's. Though he knew little about the Dark Continent, he was favourably impressed by the anti-imperialist rhetoric of the generation of African postcolonial leaders. A few days before Ghana became the first black African colony to win independence in March 1957, Khrushchev declared enthusiastically, "The awakening of the peoples of Africa has begun." A Soviet correspondent at the Conference of Independent Africa States a year later reported with equal enthusiasm that Africa has spoken for the first time in her history! The KGB, however, still paid little attention. Not until the summer of 1960, when Khrushchev decided to attend the next session of the United Nations to welcome the admission of sixteen newly independent African states, did the FCD establish a department to specialize in sub-Saharan Africa.

As well as enjoying his own dozen lengthy speeches to the general assembly in the autumn of 1960, Khrushchev must also have relished the passionate denunciations of Western imperialism by African leaders such as Kwame Nkrumah who declared that the flowing tide of African nationalism sweeps everything before it and constitutes a challenge to the colonial powers to make a just restitution for the years of injustice and crime committed against our

51

continent . . . For years and years Africa has been the footstool of colonialism and imperialism, exploitation and degradation. From the north to the south, from the east to the west, her sons languished in the chains of slavery and humiliation, and Africa's exploiters and self-appointed controllers of her destiny strode across our land with incredible inhumanity, without mercy, without shame, and without honour.

Though describing himself as an African socialist rather than a Marxist-Leninist, Nkrumah endorsed Lenin's analysis of imperialism as the 'highest stage of capitalism,' still intent on exploiting post-colonial Africa. He claimed Lenin's authority for arguing that 'neo-colonialism . . . can be more dangerous to our legitimate aspirations of freedom and economic independence than outright political control':

[Neo-colonialism] acts covertly, manoeuvring men and governments, free of the stigma attached to political rule. It creates client states, independent in name but in point of fact pawns of the colonial power is supposed to have given them independence. This is one of [what Lenin called] the divers forms of dependent countries which, politically, are formally independent, but, in fact, are enmeshed in the net of financial and diplomatic dependence.[8]

The outcome? Western chose tyrants, autocrats, or despots who ruled by the gun replaced many or all these leaders. One of the earliest among these military leaders was Mobutu Sese Seko. His role in Central Africa was preeminent to the Western cause—commissioned by the West; he was the distributor of weapons bound for Savimbi's pro-Western UNITA rebel movement and pro-Western insurgencies in many other countries in Africa. "In July, President Ford and his 'Forty Committee,' which oversaw covert action, authorized large-scale CIA covert support for the FNLA and UNITA through Zaire and Zambia, both hostile to the MPLA."[9] It was not a surprise then that Mobutu had a red-carpet reception in the United States following the perestroika as a way of the master he had served so well, thanking him for a job well done.

CHAPTER SIX

Racism, Discrimination, and Realpolitik

"It is now up to you, gentlemen, to show that you are worthy of our confidence?" This was the most incredulous and unreasonable demand Europeans made of Africa at the dawn of freedom. They would make similar demands of Africans after slavery all over Western nations where they found themselves because of slavery. The European was quick to call them idlers and a classless people just after slavery and segregation in the West and after slavery and colonialism in Africa.

If Africans have innate cruelty as some Western media and politicians portray, Europeans could not have subdued them in the first place. Because the Europeans came to Africa in small numbers at first, they could not have lived to tell their stories of discoveries if their hosts had innate cruelty. The Africans could have murdered every one of them as they came. For such is the instinct of evildoers—to take advantage of every opportunity to do evil deeds.

And routing these early Europeans was possible regardless of their maxim and gunboat,[10] historians' favourite in a list of disadvantages that succumbed Africans to European dehumanization. Ancient African kingdoms had about, at least, one hundred thousand people including great armies per kingdom; they could have routed the Europeans just by their overwhelming numbers.

Nonetheless, the strangers took advantage of the black man's kindness, such as the reason behind the Boer settlement in South Africa. A people who were passing on, but ran out of fresh water and fresh vegetables, then came ashore, only to finally take the African lands. They seeped in as religious/missionary, humanitarian and educator impostors and overcome the African people. It was too late for Africans, who would only become astonished by this so-called good faith stranger's wrath. "Does the white man understand our customs about land? How can he when he does not even speak our tongue?"[11]

The Africans did not commit such heinous crimes against people of other races anywhere in the world such as the Europeans enslaved Africans for four hundred years and continue to plunder Africa as I write. Africans did not institute such draconian rule to demean people of another race as Europeans against the Africans in many, many years of apartheid in South Africa. Nor did they commit such beastly crimes against another race as the Europeans against Africans in Congo's ivory-and-rubber gathering, against Africans in Firestone rubber plantation in Liberia, against Africans in France's colonial war of Algeria, and against the Jews in WWII.

Because of Europeans' immoral act against their female slaves in the past, many Africans meet a brick wall in search of their patrilineal ancestries today. This is because Europeans used African women as slaves by day and mistresses at night. No social animal turns it back from its young for feeling of superiority over mother and young. Raping of subjects and slaves was rampant in the colonies as well as on Western plantations in the epochs of slavery and colonialism.

The new wave of genealogical testing also has reopened one of America's ugliest wounds by confirming with science what historians have contended for generations: In slavery times and beyond, large numbers of black women were impregnated by white slave owners or other white men in positions of power.

About 30% of black Americans who take DNA tests to determine their African lineage prove to be descended from Europeans on their father's side, says Rick Kittles, scientific director of African Ancestry, a Washington, D.C., company that began offering the tests in 2003. Almost all black Americans whom Kittles has tested descended from African women, he says.[12]

Many racist European immoral acts against Africans are well documented. Late Dr. Frantz Fanon was a psychiatrist who served in colonial Algeria during the war for independence. He saw, recorded, and treated "symptoms of mental disorders of the reactionary type"[13] in both Africans and European fighters. Among many of such cases, Dr. Fanon gave an account of a patient who suffered "impotence following the rape of his wife."[14] His wife told him they could no longer continue being married because she had been dishonoured—French soldiers repeatedly raped her.

Despite brutality against Africans in Algeria, European scientists argued and concluded unanimously that North Africans have an innate tendency to commit violence. "The Algerian frequently kills other men . . . The Algerian kills savagely . . . The Algerian kills for no reason."[15] These were the scientific facts the colonial administration would cling unto in dealing with the Algerians for many years.

Professor A. Porot, a mental health specialist and neurologist, developed the following theory: The Algerian is "complete or almost complete lack of emotivity. Credulous and susceptible to the extreme. Persistent obstinacy. Mental puerility, without the spirit of curiosity found in the Western child."[16] In 1935, he defined his theory, "The native of North Africa, whose superior and cortical activities are only slightly developed, is primitive creature whose life, essentially vegetative and instinctive, is above all regulated by his diencephalons."[17] He further called North African primitivism and criminality in the *Southern Medical and Surgical*

Gazette as a "social condition, which has reached the limit of its evolution."[18] He contrasted it to the Westerner and compared it to the beast, "It is logically adapted to a life different from ours . . . The Algerian has no cortex: or, more precisely, he is dominated, like the inferior vertebrates, by the diencephalons."[19]

This study was based on fallacious scientific logic. Evidence that supported the premise included acts of violence committed by those disillusioned by colonialists' violence. Dr. Fanon argued this point, "Criminality impulses found in North Africans which have their origin in the national war of liberation."[20] In the fifties, Professor Porot collaborated with another study performed in East Africa where the ruthless Mau Mau war against colonialism had begun in 1951. The conclusion was obvious, but it served the colonial masters well to justify brutality against his so-called atavistic savages who were resistant to Western civilization.

But the most damning report came from Dr. A. Carothers, an expert from the World Health Organization (WHO), who would argue a striking similarity between the African and the lobotomized European. Coming from a WHO official, African students had to study this hard-to-swallow, fallacious scientific conclusion for decades. Such dehumanizing of Africans in psychological preparedness for Western imperialism and ideological warfare was a blow to Pan-Africanists who sought to rule their own people.

Before him, George Washington Williams, son of a freed slave, minister, lawyer, and journalist went to King Leopold II's ironic "Congo Free State" against His Majesty's will. From there, he reported for the world, among many atrocities he saw first-hand Europeans were committing against the black man, "White traders and state officials were kidnapping African women and using them as concubines."[21] From his report, the world would coin such phrase as "crimes against humanity." Many of such other unreported cases led to many fatherless babies all over colonial Africa, Europe, and the Americas.

Some people may argue that these works were scientific flaws, but to show that such studies have racial overtones in them is to turn to the notorious Tuskegee Experiment[22] for which President Clinton apologized in May 16, 1997:

The United States Government did something that was wrong, deeply, profoundly, morally wrong. It was an outrage to our commitment to integrity and equality for all our citizens. We can end the silence. We can stop turning our heads away. We can look at you in the eye and finally say on behalf of the American people what the United States Government did was shameful, and I am sorry.[23]

As a matter of wrongdoing, the apartheid regime of South Africa tortured, murdered, and massacred Africans while Europe and United States looked on. Its white minority government authorities locked Nelson Mandela up in prison for twenty-seven years, the man UN Secretary General Kofi A. Annan would write about, "To this day, Madiba[24] remains probably the single most admired, most respected international figure in the entire world."[25] But that is just one show of Africans' resilience to spring back in shape against all odds.

There is an array of evidence to show that Europeans blatantly and perpetually did injustice to others for implied superiority and economic reasons even where their lives and well-being were not under threat. Nelson Mandela cherished an ideal of equal right for all South Africans regardless of race throughout his political struggle against apartheid. He spoke in his emotional opening speech of the Rivonia Trial, Pretoria Supreme Court, on 20 April 1964:

During my lifetime I have dedicated myself to this struggle of the African people. I have fought against white domination, and I have fought against black domination. I have cherished the ideal of a democratic and free society in which all persons live together in harmony and with equal opportunities. It is an ideal, which I hope to live for and to achieve. But if needs be, it is an ideal for which I am prepared to die.[26]

Apparently, that ideal did not prevent him from being incarcerated for twenty-seven years in Robin Island prison. Europeans mass murdered millions of Jews, their own kind too, baking them in ovens in WWII. Europeans murdered over twenty million African men and women and light-skinned Africans in the Congo and Algeria wars combined.

In fact, the world first knew of hacking human limbs not in Sierra Leone, but in King Leopold II's war against Africans for plunder in Congo Free State. The Congo Free State was an oxymoron for "Congo Cruel State" where white officials reduced the killing of the black man to a mere game. Again, we shall visit William's crimes against humanity report for an insight, "The officers made a wager of £5 that they could hit the native with their rifles. Three shots were fired and the native fell dead, pierced through the head."[27]

Williams being an African American, there is no doubt his report reached the United States government. But the United States continued its blind support for King Leopold II's Congo Free State through advocacy from then chairman of senate foreign committee, Senator John Tyler Morgan, who would argue on the senate floor, "Africa was prepared for the Negro as certainly as the Garden of Eden was prepared for Adam and Eve . . ." Indeed, Congo Free State was a Garden of Eden for the black man where the forbidden trees flourished in rubber plantations that bore forbidden fruits such as Mobutu of DR Congo, Charles Taylor of Liberia, Foday Sankoh of Sierra Leone, and the leaders of Sudan, Rwanda and Burundi, Angola, etc..

And we saw in recent years how the United States benefited from its support of King Leopold II's massacre of the native Congolese; Belgium tossed Congo over to the U.S.

government. The latter in turn domesticated a bulldog in the person of Mobutu Sese Seko[28] in a manifest anger against his people for thirty years. Mobutu, too, must have been a history student of King Leopold II to understand how much pleasure is in having a hired harem of prostitutes in a dictator's hotel room in the West. "Leopold had paid £800 a month, a former servant of the house testified, for a steady supply of young women, some of whom were ten to fifteen years old and guaranteed to be virgins."[29] It was not surprising then when news broke out that Mobutu was womanizing in Paris's five-star hotels.

Like King Leopold II, Mobutu "made no distinction between state assets and his own; in a single year, he ferry five thousand long-haired sheep to his ranch at Gbadolite. While his yacht was being renovated in 1987, he simply took over the most comfortable of the few remaining passenger boats still operating on the river system."[30] Such is the Western civilization African leaders inherited, Africanists historians refused to call as is.

It is interesting how Hochschild, in his book, *King Leopold's Ghost,* unveiled Leopold's shroud only to find Mobutu inside. Yet the world judges African people by Western-initiated or sponsored corruption, conflicts, and civil wars such as Hutu/Tutsi, Liberia, Sierra Leone, DR Congo, and many more. It must be due to narcissism and racism to turn around and claim that Africans are full of innate cruelty.

Further yet, the HIV/AIDS drug nevirapine controversy in HIVNET 012[31] clinical research recently alarmed Africans copiously. The controversy surrounds Dr. Jonathan M. Fishbein, a medical doctor and pharmaceutical clinical researcher who was the director of the Office for Policy Clinical Research Operations (OPCRO) at the Division of AIDS (DAIDS), an arm of the National Institute of Health (NIH). NIH officials claimed they fired Dr. Fishbein because of poor performance, but a *Washington Post* article stated, "Fishbein said NIH is trying to fire him in retaliation for his refusal to overlook shortcomings in research practices, including not obtaining proper informed consent, in NIH-sponsored studies of the drug nevirapine on African research subjects."[32]

Institutionalized racism against Africans in the past, including using them as a guinea pig in medical research, are reasons for alarm. And many people are now comparing the HIVNET 012 research to the notorious Tuskegee Experiment of the past. The following is a background on nevirapine and HIVNET 012 study, the drug in the study to prevent HIV transmission in childbirth that sparked the controversy.

Nevirapine was approved in the United States in June 1996, for use in combination with other antiretroviral for treating HIV. For this use, it is taken twice a day for as long as the virus is under control.

Later, a study in Uganda from 1997 to 1999 (the HIVNET 012 clinical trial) found that a single dose of nevirapine given to the mother and a single dose to the infant reduced HIV transmission (from childbirth or breastfeeding) during the first fourteen to sixteen weeks of life to about half of what it was with a very short course of AZT. This study in 645 mother-infant pairs, conducted as collaboration between researchers from Johns Hopkins University and Uganda and funded by the U.S. National Institutes of Health (NIH), was published in September 1999. It showed that HIV transmission at childbirth could be greatly reduced by a very inexpensive and easy regimen even when the mother had little or no prenatal care. It is rightly considered one of the great successes in HIV prevention.

Nevirapine alone is not the best regimen, however. Later it was learned from the same study that even the single dose sometimes selects for resistance mutations in the mother's HIV—a serious problem because it could make her treatment more difficult in the future. This can be prevented by treating the mother's HIV if she needs antiretroviral treatment, which of course should be done anyway—or by using a much more difficult regimen of AZT to prevent transmission—or by adding other drugs (usually AZT plus 3TC) to suppress the virus while the nevirapine is slowly eliminated from the body. But still today, the great majority of women with HIV do not have access to any antiretroviral treatment. Single-dose nevirapine is inexpensive and easy to use—and in some areas, many women will not accept a longer course of medication because they are afraid of the consequences if people around them learn or suspect that they have HIV.[33]

We may not know the truth about HIVNET 012 study in 645 mother-infant pairs in Uganda until it is as late as the Tuskegee Experiment. Simply, they cannot reverse the clinical research. If Dr. Fishbein's wrongdoing and cover-up claims were true, obviously they would remain cover-up to protect the face of a Western institution from embarrassment. For the West, 645 times two plus more[34] mothers and infants languishing in Africa is preferable to any embarrassment the truth may cause NIH and the United States. Needless to wonder that proponents of the research are calling Dr. Fishbein a disgruntled employee of NIH. But the same National Institute of Allergy and Infectious Diseases (NIAID), an arm of NIH had awarded Dr. Fishbein "in Appreciation of Outstanding Contribution and Efforts in Support of the NIAID Mission," certificate in November 2003. So far, we can only look at e-mail communications between Dr. Fishbein's bosses in the run-up to his termination:

From: Hochensmith, Robert[35] (NIH/NIAID)
RHochensmith@niaid.nih.gov
To: Kagan, Jonathan M.[36] (NIH/NIAID)
JKAGAN@niaid.nih.gov
Sent: Fri Feb 13 08:12:27 2004
Subject: RE: T—42[37] and probation

Jon,

Dr. Fishbein was also recommended for an award so if you are thinking about moving on termination you may want to pull the award recommendation." Back and forth, exchanges between the two continue on the same thread and on the same day. Kagan: "Thanks Bob." Robert: "Yes. He is on an indefinite appointment but has a 2-year initial probationary period, which began on 17/13/03[38] when hired. The IC may terminate during the trial period because of his work performance or conduct during this period if he fails to demonstrate fitness or qualifications for continued employment. Terminating his employment would require notifying him in writing as to why he is being separated and the effective date of the action. THERE IS NO APPEAL AVAILABLE FOR EMPLOYEES WHO ARE REMOVED DURING THEIR TRIAL PERIOD.

Bob.

Kagan: Blunt question. Does Fishbein have a probationary period? I beg you to say yes. And/or, I assume he has an indefinite T-24 contract, right? How hard would it be to terminate that? Will discuss in-person with you if preferred. Thanks.

However, NIH officials have not provided much evidence to counter Dr. Fishbein's damning claims against NIH and NIH-sponsored HIVNET 012 study, which he has referred to as a reckless medical research in Africa. In another instance, he wrote, "By the new NIH standard it is now permissible to visit upon people in third world countries research too substandard to the treatment of Americans." And those people in the third world countries he was referring to were the Africans in the NIVNET 012 study, the upright scientific variables.

When Dr. Smith, a safety expert, called Edmond Tramont's[39] attention to "the lack of adherence to serious adverse event reporting requirement, the poor quality of subject records, the failure of the study staff to use the proper toxicity grading scales, and the absence of staff supervision and quality control," he suppressed her document and argued "his opinion that Africans in the midst of an AIDS crisis deserved some leniency in meeting U.S. safety standards." Besides the show of invectiveness against Dr. Fishbein, we see in Hochensmith capitalized closing sentence in the e-mail above, there is no mention of a clear-cut reason for termination being plotted. The generalized use of "his work performance or conduct" does not tell us much. In a separate e-mail discussion, Lisa Poindexter wrote to Lynn Hellinger:[40]

Our T-42 employees serve a two years probationary period. The Division Directors agreed upon 2 years instead of one to allow adequate time to assess the employee's performance. This policy was publicized in the briefing materials back in 2001 and we have been following the practice. However, I now need to develop a formal policy document and have Dr. Fauci[41] sign it.

The unfortunate thing is that I am having a hard time trying to locate the OPF. The file room does have some paperwork on him, but they have indicated that they never received the OPF. Thus, I cannot locate the probationary letter for Dr. Fishbein. The EHRP system does have Dr. Fishbein on probation until July 2005. He came on board in July 2003.

According to the NIH policy document, we can terminate the employee serving a probationary period because his work performance or conduct during the period fails to demonstrate fitness or qualifications for continued employment.

We must notify the employee in writing as to why he is being separated and the effective date of the action. At a minimum, the memo should consist of the IC's conclusions as to the inadequacies of his/her performance or conduct.

Still a generalization of "he/her" when the employee in question is a "he." On the other hand, Dr. Fishbein's records speak loudly on his behalf. In his committee on reviewing the HIVNET 012 Prenatal HIV Prevention Trial Board on Health Promotion and Disease Prevention Institute of Medicine National Academies of Sciences hearing in January 4, 2005, Dr. Fishbein stated his qualifications and experience.[42]

Indeed, this nevirapine HIVNET 012 research controversy has opened up a complete complex issue for concerned Africans. It is still unclear whether the controversy emanated out of grudge at NIH or Dr. Fishbein is acting out of selflessness.[43] Combing through some of the information resources available at the time of writing so far has failed to answer critical questions.

I spoke to twenty HIV/AIDS clinics and doctors and asked the following question: "Is there a single dose antiretroviral drug available for pregnant women in the United States that prevents or minimizes transmission of HIV virus to unborn infants?" The answer was yes from the clinics and doctors. But to the follow-up question whether the choice of drug was nevirapine, the answer turned out to be not nevirapine. All of them told me the drug of choice was Retrovir, whose generic name is called zidovudine. To ensure there was no confusion between the brand names, nevirapine (Viramune) and zidovudine (Retrovir), I asked twenty drug store pharmacists the same questions, and they all came up with the same answers.

This is my finding including all the literature and news coverage about the controversy. Now the questions remain; we now know of the difficulty in treating mothers' HIV in the aftermath of nevirapine treatment. NIH, NIAD researchers, and the DHHS[44] categorically stated that there is no cover-up about that fact. It is also understood that the AIDS virus mutation causes difficulty in treatment, which could be minimized by further treatment with expensive antiretroviral drugs cocktail. We also know that Africa does not have the resources to administer such expensive follow-up treatment to its HIV/AIDS patients. It is also a given fact that nevirapine is the drug of choice because of its inexpensiveness. What we do not know is whether there is a clear-cut plan to make available a follow-up treatment to the experiment group who cannot afford the follow-up treatment themselves. Would these mothers and their neonates be abandoned as in Tuskegee Experiment?

Normally, it would make sense to perform such experiment in a country where a follow-up treatment is available and affordable. Was the experiment performed in Africa because the United States does not have enough HIV/AIDS victims to carry it out? Why the drug of choice for the same purpose in the United States is zidovudine and nevirapine in Africa? For help with these many dead-end questions, I turned to a notable doctor and researcher in the African community, Aiah A. Gbakima, PhD, Department of Biology, Spencer Hall, G12, Morgan State University, Baltimore, who is now the principal and vice chancellor of the University of Sierra Leone for help and the following is his contribution:

The answer to your question: "Nevirapine Mis-information: Will It Kill?" is yes.

Nevirapine will kill if long-term treatment is not correctly and vigorously monitored in certain patients, particularly in female patients infected with HIV and with CD4 cell counts of <250 cell/mm3.[45] What is Nevirapine?

Viramune is the brand name for nevirapine (NVP), a non-nucleoside reverse transcriptase inhibitor with activity against Human Immunodeficiency Virus Type1 (HIV-1). Nevirapine is structurally a member of the dipyrido-diazepinone chemical class of compounds (Boehringer Ingelheim, 2005)." According to this document, severe, life-threatening, and in some cases fatal hepatotoxicity, particularly in the first 18 weeks, has been reported in patients treated with viramune. Female gender and higher

CD4 cell counts at initiation of therapy place patients at increased risk. Women with CD4 counts <250 cell/mm3, including pregnant women receiving viramune in combination with other antiretroviral for the treatment of HIV infection are at the greatest risk. However, the report goes to say that, "Hepatotoxicity associated with viramune can occur in both genders, all CD4 counts and at any time during treatment."

While the CD4 counts <250 cells/mm3 is the main determinant for hepatotoxicity, clearly, women are at a greater risk than men are. But another report from FDA says that liver toxicity occurs with long term use of nevirapine (viramune),[46] and although nevirapine-related deaths due to symptomatic liver toxicity, including some in HIV-infected pregnant women, serious and fatal liver toxicity has not been reported after a single doses of nevirapine.

The problems with the NIH project HIVNET 012 protocol were many folds. Firstly, we are not very sure if the local members of the study team were properly trained to undertake and monitor such a very sensitive and complex clinical trial study and this has been highlighted in some of the reviews from inside NIH itself. Secondly, in such a study, the views of all staff should be taken very seriously, discussed and some measure of compromise to be reached before the next phase of the study should have begun. But, that seem not to have happened. In fact, the changing of the review by another person to facilitate the re-opening of the site that had visible monitoring problems was grossly inappropriate for scientific integrity. NIH sets the standards for integrity for human protection during scientific research, which includes clinical trials. One should lead by example. Having said that, I do not believe that these were done intentionally, but that they did this to get more funding for a project that the NIH scientists thought was going to be a major public health break through. In fact, there were deaths amongst both the neonates and mothers, but it seems that the deaths took place long after delivery of the children.

Dr. Fishbein should not lose his job because he was critical of the HIVNET 012 study. On the contrary, he should be encouraged to be critical, because internal scrutiny is an important factor for human protection in such cases. He is doing what they employed him to do and this is the same thing that should apply to Dr. Graham's criticism of the FDA's handling of the vioxx issue.

The lessons we in the developing nations should learn from this and other studies is that we should be a major part of these studies from day one and we should not allow ourselves to be sucked in by the dollar amounts and forget that our people may be hurt by such studies. Above all, we should be very vigilant and critical of all the activities. If that means, being critical on your own very study, then, so be it, but human subject must be protected in medical research.

There is no doubt that nevirapine is a good drug of choice to prevent the transmission of HIV from mother to child, but the protocols should be studied carefully and revised many times to provide answers to many of the nagging questions that may refuse to die. There is a place for clinical trials as they provide important information on the use of drugs. In this case, this treatment regimen has proved very useful.

My personal view,
Aiah A. Gbakima Baltimore, MD

We should not allow ourselves to be sucked in by the dollar amounts and forget that our people may be hurt by such studies. I found Dr. Gbakima's comment rather interesting. Could it be that some Ugandan officials are being sucked in by the almighty dollar bills? As I said, we may never know because of the golden rule: the owner of the dollar bills tells the story.

Recently, Mrs. Bush, former president George Bush Senior's wife, after touring the Astrodome complex in Houston, where Hurricane Katrina victims were crammed, made a comment on American Public Media program

(*Marketplace*): "What I'm hearing, which is sort of scary, is they all want to stay in Texas. Everyone is so overwhelmed by the hospitality. And so many of the people in the arena here, you know, were underprivileged anyway, so this is working very well for them." She was speaking of displaced persons the United States media had been calling all along refugees in their own country because majority of them were poor people from minority groups and further yet most were black people. And around the same time, William Bennett, who has held prominent posts in the administrations of former president Ronald Reagan and George Bush, made a comment on the Salem Radio Network, "If you wanted to reduce crime, you could—if that were your sole purpose— you could abort every black baby in this country and your crime rate would go down."

Although the media got it right what Mrs. Bush meant, "The people were better off at the complex before Hurricane Katrina." She further revealed that without Katrina, the world would not have known of the subhuman condition many poor black people are being systematically subjected to in a great nation as the United States, especially under her son's watch of a group of Republican "neocons" regime. No surprise if these people were overwhelmed by the hospitality in a crammed stadium complex under displaced persons' status. But that of Bennett's comment was so obvious it just crowned the racist undertone in both comments.

Such is how Europeans have been mindless of the prerequisites that ascend people to a bourgeoisie class, which, of course, do not come to them automatically, especially that the same Europeans had rubbed Africans and African Americans of their dignity in the epochs of slavery, colonialism, imperialism, apartheid, and segregation only to turn around to make such unreasonable demands.

From the time Europeans stumbled upon Africa in the fifteenth century to the second half of the twentieth century, Africans had endured a steady persecution in that period.

What we now know as economic and political imperialism or economic colonization, as Lumumba put it, followed this period to the present day.

Western nations must desist from policies of realpolitik in Africa first, if Africa must live by the expectations of King Baudouin of Belgium when in Leopoldville, on granting Congo freedom, stated, "It is now up to you, gentlemen, to show that you are worthy of our confidence."[47] Contrarily, the West invariably chokes Africa economically through dubious economic and subversive political policies to protect economic interests. Surely, notwithstanding massive corruption among many African leaders, Western economic policies and political subversion in Africa more so expose the latter to the need of asking for handouts.

Western interference with politics and economics in Africa is hurting Africa way more than the four hundred years of slaving, raping, killing, and plundering. Bad loans are a clear evidence of their dubious economic policies. These loans are riddled with fine prints of unfair trade and lending practices for already blindfolded by economic strangulation and anxious African leaders—extreme high interest rates and crooked international trade agreements. To understand this properly is to study its microcosm that has for the most part stunted the growth of Africans who found themselves in the West because of slavery or economic migration.

The internal lending practices demand that the lenders establish the creditors' capacity to pay back, which include criteria that establish the creditors' residential, employment, and financial stability. There are laws that protect the debtors should creditors fail to follow these guidelines including, in the United States, bankruptcy laws that are designed to relieve them from the clutches of predatory lending merchants. Various jargons explain this: chapter 7, chapter 11 chapters 13, and so on. Nevertheless, the debtors have to be educated about such protection. This mostly places the African Americans at the disadvantage, who, less than hundred years ago, only went to school at the will of their masters and about fifty years ago went to ill-equipped segregated schools.

Nonetheless, Western banks representatives come to Africa, give loans to unstable, ill-educated leaders, undemocratic, sometimes despotic governments and military regimes at international level, and pass them on to children unborn, cloaked in high loan maintenance cost that go on forever to repay. This is one of the impediments to Africa's economic development: loan maintenance to Western banking institutions.

For example, under the government of Prime Minister Siaka Stevens in 1970, Sierra Leone's then selfless bank governor, Dr. Mohamed Sorrie Forna warned Stevens and nations of the world: "Finally, let me warn the nations of the World that should their citizens allow you to embark on a pre-finance spree in the terminal days of your regime this nation reserves the right to disallow these debts in the future."[48]

The West must write off these bad loans. They approved these loans not based on good banking practices, but on sentiment to despots and dictators for doing their bidding. If they refuse, Africans must demand they refund the billions of dollars they stole from Africa through slave labour in ivory, rubber, produce and mineral gathering and mining. Africans must also demand they pay restitution for crimes against humanity they committed in Africa. David Quammen in his well-written article in the *National Geographic* magazine, "Tracing the Human Footprint," wrote,

Anyone who listens can detect those notes. Africans want better and fuller employment. They want food security and education for their children. They want good governance, free of oppression and corruption. They want fair, sensible arrangements for the management of wild landscapes and natural resources—arrangements chosen and controlled by Africans. They want peace. They're proud to be African as well as proud to be Dogon or Fang or Tuareg or Samburu or

Tutsi, to be Kenyan or Ghanaian or Gabonese. Directly or indirectly, they suffer from the widespread ravages of AIDS, the pressures of population growth, and the broadly ramifying crush of poverty. Old-fashioned colonialism is most gone, but its thefts and damages haven't been well rectified.[49]

Make no mistake; writing off these bad loans is not a gift or another handout to Africa. They were monies the West stole from Africa. There is no way to begin to calculate how much human and economic loss Africa suffered to European cruelty and plundering in the epochs of slavery, colonialism, and bad loan maintenance or even to try to calculate financial loss. How will Africa progress when the West unchained the necks and ankles of Africans and handed the chains to international banking institution to chain Africans to the IMF and the World Bank vaults? Africans have to work hard on farms and deep mining to produce raw material to support Western factories in an unfair exchange. Writing off these bad loans would only jump-start Africa in its new political and economic systems its fine scholars will scion design to soothe the culture and tradition of its peoples.

Besides Western policies of realpolitik, at the dawn of independence in Africa, there were few graduates per independence state with daunting responsibility on them to lead their people on only one track: foreign political and economic systems. Many post-independence African leaders who looked elsewhere outside this realm met a similar fate as Patrice Lumumba and his government. It is obvious how foreign ideals failed Africa miserably. There must be another and a better track. There is no magic wand to this problem, but a thinking hat for the black man to shake off international capitalism, to shake off international socialism, and to shake off international communism. Africa has allowed others to fight over its political conscience for too long.

Thus, over half of the conflicts in Africa had\have direct links to European attempts to eradicate the despots who they had imposed on Africans during the cold war. At a time when the world operated in this sphere of ideological influence, the tendency for African countries' political scale to tip toward communism was high. Absolute tyrants, autocrats, and despots were desirable then to stall communism from gaining grounds in Africa. This was meted in various forms and degrees: tyrants replaced monarchs, autocrats replaced aristocrats and evil political systems as in apartheid or despotic military regimes, and depending on the nature of local politics in these various countries were entrenched. In essence, the cold war warriors denied Africans a freedom of choice of political ideological alignment following independence. And the victorious Western nations are now saying to their African thugs "the war is over and you are no longer needed" in a new tug-of-war among Western European countries. One classical example is in the Great Lake region where France and the United States locked horns in the new scramble for Africa in 1994 and 1997 that left about a million African casualties in its aftermath—now for economic interest. "In Rwanda, Zaire, and other countries, Christopher, Albright, Berger, the CIA, a newly-assertive DIA, the U.S. Special Operations Command, and American Mercenaries, would have their bloodied fingerprints on yet more massacres, official lies, and clandestine military operations."[50] In all these struggles, democracy was a far-fetched concept to go by, nonetheless, good polity, which seems to have prevailed in Africa before the political brouhaha.

Besides the Republic of South Africa, the West is head-on with the despots who now need restraint. South Africa's apartheid regime was clever to understand it could no longer remain cloaked in communism. Apartheid had become useless to Western powers—and the realization dawned on its leadership that Western powers were only interested in keeping communists in their abbey, in the Soviet Union, where it crumbled on them in one place. "The crumbling of the Soviet system ultimately did far more than Soviet Cold War policy to persuade the apartheid regime that its time was up."[51] Nonetheless, South Africa appears to be the only success story for communism in Africa. Even Andrew and Mitrokhin agree, "The only Africa country which arguably represented something of a KGB success story was South Africa. Though the African National Congress (ANC) was never at any point the Communist stooge which the apartheid regime liked to pretend, Soviet support, channelled through the KGB, helped sustain it in some of its darkest hours."[52]

Meanwhile, the rest of African leaders have tasted power, and it has intoxicated them. And they are poised to resist their masters' effort to barter oligarchy aristocracy, tyranny, monarchy, or autocracy for democracy. Democracy, the favourable form of governments, has been put on hold throughout the cold war; and the offspring of this tug-of-war to swap them once more are pro-Communist/pro-Western leaders such as Savimbi, Mobutu, Botha, and so on. In fact, Jacques Foccart, who was commonly known as Monsieur Afrique, the water boy for Charles de Gaulle of France, had his own kingmaker military. He would later boast in his memoirs of handpicking the longest lasting dictator and one of the most ruthless despots of Africa, Omar Bongo of Gabon and self-pronounced Emperor Jean-Bédel Bokassa of Central African Republic.

When Gabon's president Leon M'ba was overthrown by opposition forces in 1964, Foccart organized a French military expedition that returned him to power. According to his 1995 memoirs (Foccart Speaks), which many observers thought were purposely annotated awaiting publication of his full memoirs after his death, Foccart claimed to have personally selected Omar Bongo as M'ba successor in Gabon. He was said to have conducted what was essentially a job interview of Bongo over dinner. Foccart boasted that he permitted the 1966 coup in Central Africa Republic which brought to power Jean-Bédel Bokassa, who later pronounced himself "emperor" of the nation and participated in rites of cannibalism.[53]

But hooliganism would soon follow when the people rose against these pro-Communist/pro-Western puppets: Charles Taylor and Foday Sankoh and many more are neonates of such hooliganism turned hardened rebels.

Seemingly, the creation of Frankenstein such as Foday Sankoh and other warlords around Africa was systematic not only in Africa, but also in many former Western empires. Western colonial masters were opponents in empire acquisition, but united in dissemination of political ideology in the aftermath of colonialism. Thus, economic and political imperialism followed colonialism. Dissimilar to colonialism, political ideologues had a parallel motivation in Africa, which was mainly to spread political ideology that will enable the raping of the continent's wealth of raw materials—an economic duopoly between Eastern and Western Europe. Their only differences were in empire acquisition, later ideology—communism versus capitalism and now economic imperialism among West European nations.

Former Union of Soviet Socialist Republics (USSR) did not possess colonies in Africa. The fact remained that communism and capitalism were in a political contest for influence in Africa after independence. In an attempt to bring down communism, Western nations waged a war on Pan-Africanists, many of whom were leaning to leftist ideology, to hold on to their former empires. This was what set the endless mushroom of wars in gear, in Africa, on the following two tracks: those rebels in capitalist boots set out to clean after Western powers and those democracy-seeking men who have no business in leadership. Socrates explained the latter better in the following philosophical dialogue at Cephalos's house where he attempted to argue how nations become failed states:

The aristocratic constitution degenerates into the timocratic (or honour-loving) when the warrior class prevails over the wisdom-loving class, and imposes a militant policy dictated by ambition and the love of glory. Similarly, in the soul of the timocratic man, the spirited part gains precedence over the reasoning part, and the result is a valiant but contentious and ambitious nature. The timocratic constitution degenerates into oligarchy (the rule of the few) when honour-loving turns to money-grubbing. The city is divided into rich rulers and poor subjects. In the soul of the oligarchic man, pleasure-loving but ungenerous, the desiring part prevails over the reasoning and spirited parts. The oligarchic constitution degenerates into democracy (the rule of the people) when the poor in the oligarchic state revolt. All are then set free to do as they wish—and, says Socrates in effect, to go to the devil in their own way. Where the oligarchic man, thrifty at heart, gave way only to the moneymaking (or necessary) desires, the democratic man, casting off even this restraint, gives free rein to the spendthrift (or unnecessary) desires, and liberty is thus complete. The democratic constitution degenerates into tyranny when men tire at last of the lawlessness of liberty, which has become license. They appoint a strong man to restore order; he raises a bodyguard or private army to suppress the irresponsible elements in society; and, unperceived, tyranny is established in the city.[54]

Such is how Western nations induced these many wars in Africa during and after the cold war. Efforts to correct previous ill political dealings really went bad, which are now causing these many wars. But the West, the lion's share perpetrator of political subversion in Africa has turned a blind eye to the problems. Now to make a downright mockery of Africa, Western powers send intervention forces everywhere there are wars along Caucasus Mountains' corridors. These include countries of the former communist bloc that Africa helped Western nations to acquire in the cold war. Western politicians acclaim peacekeeping or intervention troops, "good show boys" accolades for successive peacekeeping or interventions in these conflicts. On the other hand, swarms of journalists hurry to Africa to indulge in yellow journalism for television amusement.

These politicians in turn sit around conference tables abounded by such good old Washington inflections, "African solutions to African problems," oversimplifying the tribulations. They discuss copious not how to set Africa back on the track of real self-rule, which they had derailed it from, from the outset, the white man contacted the black man. Instead, they coin and throw phrases at each other such as "innate cruelty" stoically, referring to Africans.

CHAPTER SEVEN

Central and West Africa

The rebel war, which had begun in Liberia, would spread to Sierra Leone. It is hard to understand how Charles Taylor, a suspect of corruption who was awaiting extradition to Liberia, broke from a Massachusetts prison facility (so the U.S. government claims). Worse yet he became the head of the serpent that slithered across West Africa—a rebel leader that had much authority and an arsenal of sophisticated weapons to destabilize the whole region.

This induces further pondering over the role of Washington in the rebel conflict in Liberia. What is more is the following irony: Charles Taylor's bed-fellowship later with one of Washington's harsh enemies in the person of Col. Muammar al-Qaddafi of Libya. Many believe that this strange relationship prolonged the civil war in Liberia for the fifteen years it lasted.

Did Charles Taylor unknowingly become a double agent whom Washington would later divorce and wanted to put down, which probably added further fuel to an existing flame in the civil war? Of course, Charles Taylor was mystified to be freed from jail. But Taylor's actions and involvement with Qaddafi probably mystified the CIA even more. But the people of the region seemed to be mystified the most; the United States' possible involvement in the conflict was hardly discussed. The reason is simple: the United States and Libya could not have advanced a common cause through a common agent.

On the other hand, if Charles Taylor was indeed a double agent who enjoyed sponsorship from Washington and later Tripoli, how did he do it? It seemed like one of Washington's covert operations turned into an odd Charles Taylor, Tripoli, and Washington political love triangle. The hand that feeds is quite discernible when not blindfolded. But if the feeder spanks with the left hand and feeds with the right, it could lead to one of two reactions—either the feed is rejected or the feeder is bitten. If Washington's covert operatives to maintain secrecy had blindfolded Charles Taylor, thus, he felt no string attached when he turned to Libya for help. As well, it was probably too late if Washington had thought twice about its leadership choice in Charles Taylor for Liberia. John-Peter Pham quixotically explains the confusion about Charles Taylor's freedom from a jail in the United States in his book, *Liberia: Portrait of a Failed State*. John-Peter was either ill-informed of the truth or his account was in accord with a possible Washington cover-up. He is an American who happened to be an international diplomat in Liberia, Sierra Leone, and Guinea at the time:[1]

Taylor was arrested by U.S. marshals in Somerville, Massachusetts, on May 24, 1984, on the authority of the extradition treaty that the U.S. had with Liberia. He then spent fifteen months in prison while former U.S. Attorney-General Ramsey Clark tried to fight his extradition. When a federal court ruled that sufficient evidence existed to support the Liberian government's request for his return, Taylor escaped from the Plymouth House of Corrections, where he was being held, in September 1985. According to one report, Taylor convinced a guard to bend the rules at the facility to allow him to pass from the north wing, where he was held, to the east wing, telling the guard he wanted to play cards with a friend. Once there, he used a hacksaw blade to cut through an iron window bar and, using bed sheets tied together, he and four other inmates climbed down from the second floor, scaled a fence, and ran into the nearby woods.[2]

This would sound to a wise person like correction facilities supply hacksaws to prisoners in the United States. It is naïve to disseminate information that Taylor simply told his guard he wanted to play cards with a friend in jail only to escape afterward. Tarty Teh's essay may help us in making a logical conclusion as to what happened.

But that was then and this is now. The plan that the ACDL put forth called for recruiting Charles Taylor from prison to execute it. Taylor had a neat dictum for his mission: 'The only good Doe is a dead Doe.' In the end, President Doe and 220,000 other Liberians died. Harry Greaves spent much of that period of gruesome death and destruction on vacation from his original plan after his initial elation, expressed in dazzling prose. All that is part of our recent history. We have since screamed at one another at conferences about how to fix what was destroyed by Greaves' plan. And just when we have begun to talk to each other about what to do next, here comes Greaves with some redistribution and re-direction of already assessed blames.[3]

No doubt, Qaddafi was not happy with the United States' activity in his so-called backyard in Liberia. In a pursuit to accomplish his own agenda of eliminating a military beachhead in Africa from where he probably thought the United States obtained satellite images to bomb palaces in Libya with precision, Qaddafi was prone to support anything that would make such activity impossible in the future. And it seemed accepting help from Qaddafi was Charles Taylor's Achilles' heel in his overambitious drive to dethrone Samuel Doe who almost sounded and looked like a monarch in Liberia. The man the United States had praised when Washington made an official statement that his outright stolen of a presidential election was a progress toward democracy was now being pursued by his kingmakers.

Doe's human rights records over the years had brought shame upon Washington, yet it seemed annoying him [Doe] would have caused damage to the political, security and economic interests Washington had protected all those years in Liberia.

The race for time between Prince Johnson and Charles Taylor to kill Doe was hardly seen by average Liberians as a race between Tripoli and Washington. But it seemed that Washington had lost its man, Charles Taylor, to Libya in secrecy and must do anything to reach Doe before Qaddafi did. Otherwise, why would the most passionate nation about democracy turn its back on poor people in Liberia? How did Prince Johnson appear into the picture?

Washington, which in many cases sees nothing beyond the protection of its political and economic interests in Africa, probably created the failed state of Liberia of which John-Peter writes a well laid out over two-hundred-page book as if he too had been blindfolded to the truth.

No matter how aristocratic William Tolbert's government was, it was democratically elected by the people, it was of the people, even though it was not working in the interest of all the people, did not warrant foreign interference for its ouster". Many think that Washington turned around and supported Doe's ouster clandestinely to protect its image in world politics. Thus, Charles Taylor himself did not know he had Washington's support, who would ponder why he was released from jail to roam, freely, the streets of Massachusetts.

It indicated that Charles Taylor was not knowledgeable of Harry Greaves plan, "the plan that the ACDL put forth called for recruiting Charles Taylor from prison to execute it." Now, one could begin to connect the dots why Charles Taylor did not know not to run to Qaddafi for help.

Like the nineteenth-century American Colonization Society/International Society of the Congo, there are stunning similarities between the conflicts in West Africa and the Great Lake regions. In his testimony on April 6, 2001, roundtable conference that was organized by Ms. Cynthia McKinney, a democratic congresswoman from Georgia, USA, to discuss international investigative journalists' concerns over the link between the powerful in Washington DC and the crises in Africa, the Afro-America Network paper resonates the revelations of Wayne Madsen, an expert on intelligence and privacy issues in international investigative journalism:

He explained how, under Clinton Administration, the Rwandan Patriotic Army troops were trained by the US Administration along with the armies from Ethiopia, Uganda, and Eritrea. He added that the preparation was conducted by the US Special Forces. The National Security Agency (NSA) provided intelligence and helped in propaganda. He added that what Clinton said in Rwanda that the US Administration did not know about the Rwandan tragedy was not true. He gave the example of the US Ambassador in Burundi in 1994 who was declaring that Habyalimana's plane might have been shot down by the RPF while the Ambassador in Rwanda said the plane might have been shot down by the Hutus. He concluded that the major motives of the West in African conflicts are purely economical and that the perspectives for peace in Africa remain bleak.[4]

Wayne asserts that the United States policy in DR Congo and the Great Lake region at large "has rested, in my opinion, on the twin pillars of military aid and questionable trade. The military aid programs of the United States, largely planned and administered by the U.S. Special Operations Command and the Defense Agency (DIA), have been both overt and covert."

In Liberia, it seemed the U.S. overt and covert operations started with Doe against Tolbert in 1980 and Charles Taylor/Prince Johnson against Doe in 1989. In the DR Congo, on the other hand, were Mobutu against Lumumba in 1961, Laurence Kabila against Mobutu in 1996, and U.S. policy against Kabila in 1998 in the absence of a notable strongman. Interestingly, like Charles Taylor, who escaped from the United States prison to become a rebel leader, Ugandan officials close to Yoweri Museveni would be nabbed and charged with attempting to smuggle weapons from the United States, made a deal, after which Museveni became the U.S. point man in the Great Lake region. But he had put up $1 million bail and the $20 million value Ugandan UN Mission House as a lean to prevent the incarceration of his right-hand man, Bisangwa-Mbuguje. "In September 1992, some of Museveni's closest aides were charged with attempting to illegally smuggle 400 TOW missiles and 34 launchers from the United States to Uganda."[5]

This seemed like an established pattern; the United States government made deals with strongmen to further its cause in Africa once in the custody of its justice department. Those leaders—the presidents of Uganda, Rwanda, Ethiopia, Angola, Eritrea and Burundi, Pres. Bill Clinton's former secretary of state Madeleine Albright would call "beacon of hope" for Africa, are all former Marxist followers and military strongmen now on Western boots in the forefront of internecine capitalist war in Africa. Diamonds in Sierra Leone and columbite-tantalite or coltan, a primary component of computer microchips and printer circuit boards, in DR Congo have become a curse to both nations and subsequently to West Africa and Central Africa.

A month later following the roundtable conference, Wayne presented other stunning revelations in the United States House of Representatives hearing on May 17, 2001, on how the U.S. overt and covert operations in Central Africa aided and abated the killing of Hutu refugees by providing Rwanda and Uganda forces with military training and logistics, satellite images of Hutu refugee positions, and sometimes having foot soldiers, special operations units carrying machine guns to massacres Hutus. In every step of the way, according to Wayne, American companies were there to take full advantage of financial benefits in exploiting minerals and providing logistics. In summary of his detailed report, he told the United States House of Representatives Subcommittee on International Operations and Human Rights and Committee on International Relations:

It is beyond time for the Congress to seriously examine the role of the United States in the genocide and civil wars of central Africa, as well as the role that PMCs currently play in other African trouble spots like Nigeria, Sierra Leone, Equatorial Guinea, Angola, Ethiopia, Sudan, and Cabinda... At the very least, the United States, as the world's leading democracy, owes Africa at least the example of a critical self-inspection.[6]

These actions leave Africans pondering aloud why Africa is being treated by the West as a place where it pays to wage a war. Keita Fodeba clearly showed us in one of his greatest works of art how the misery of the African child came about in a similar way long before freedom in Africa.

In a poetic voice, Keita painted a portrait of a continent under imperialism and its impact on its people in such a vivid picture of words and music rather simplistic *African Dawn*. It is worth observing the following pointers to follow Keita's frame of mind when he wrote this rather long poem. There was a "fight between night and day" in the "African Dawn," where the rising yellow sun at dawn is the depiction of Europeans in sharp contrast with night, Africans. Observe the disappearing of the bright stars in the struggle between day and night at dawn. Only then the tragedies that abound the "African Dawn" would be demystified. Now you would surely not miss the point that like many good African leaders, Naman was among the disappearing stars of Keita's "African Dawn."

Observe that Naman's village, the apparent representation of Africa, offers the best man to the European to fight for them. Naman would not return to dance the "Douga, that sacred dance of the vultures that no one who has not performed some outstanding feat is allowed to dance, that dance of the Mali emperors of which every step is a stage in the history of the Mali race." Until one reads the Algerian war of independence, it will make little sense that Naman was conscripted to commit atrocities against his own, the African man, in the following lines that Keita punctuated by the solemn sound of the Cora when he sang, "Naman was in North Africa; he was well, and he asked for news of the harvest, of the feastings, the river, the dances, the council tree . . . in fact, for news of all the village." But not only that, Naman was sent across Europe to fight in the WWII where he became a prisoner of war.

See how Keita scion depicted the typical African families (women and children, the often victims of wars) out of Kadia under European colonialism. Kadia was happy; "Suddenly ceased grinding corn, put the mortar away under the barn." Those barns were always full of food all year round. But they were now empty when at dawn; Naman was killed like many vocal African leaders. He knew that his thinking faculty was equal to that of his commander. Nevertheless, the vulture, who feeds on only the dead, hovered above Naman in great satisfaction that it would feed of Naman's village in his absence, and Naman would be no more to dance the big dance. In this systematic way, European colonialism and imperialism deprived many good Africans from dancing that big dance, the great dance of the Douga, which has every step scion crafted after the history of Africa, after the great Manding warriors and rulers of Timbuktu.

But Africans must not be allowed to be shrouded in sorrow with folded harms, all twisted in semi-recumbent postures, and all carried away by emotions. Instead, Africans must keep ablaze the *Fire from Timbuktu*.[7]

CHAPTER EIGHT

Living on the Margins

In March 1991, the Revolutionary United Front (RUF) rebels, under a misguided leadership of Foday Sankoh,[1] waged a ruthless war on Sierra Leone, which was to last for over a decade. Sierra Leone was torn by that senseless war. The worst crimes committed against humanity in recent years also characterized the war. It seemed as portrayed by Western mass media that people turned on themselves to fulfil a natural quest and motivation for cruelty and evil intentions that had been waiting for the slightest chance to be revealed. And as if the state of anarchy was the moment to revere, the people of Sierra Leone acted like beasts in this previously unknown nation for violence, retorted by committing damnable atrocities against themselves. Indeed, such conflicts give Western journalists something to sensationalize not as outcomes of Western realpolitik and neo-colonialism in Africa, but as outcomes of African innate cruelty.

Many scholars blamed the rebel war in Sierra Leone on economic hardship compounded by "a pool of idle and disgruntled youth" that were ready for anything. That was nothing but a myopic view of the issue or a heed to slanted Western views and analysis of the rebel war. Western experts only looked at the secondary causes, which were apparent outcome of their economic policies and induced political subversion in Africa. But African scholars looked concertedly with their Western counterparts through the same lens. The latter turned the knob, zooming in as close to their noses as they could, blinding the former with broad spectrums of the closest subjects—economic hardship and "a pool of idle and disgruntled youth"—looking just at the surface of the problem. But one would ask where the economic hardship and "a pool of disgruntled youth" came from. And once the lens is knocked away, far back, is an array of events: slavery, colonialism, force labour, economic and political imperialism, economic hardship, selfish and corrupt leadership, and then "a pool of idle and disgruntled youth."

By independence, most of the human and natural resources ranging from slaves, cash crop, diamonds, and other precious minerals in Sierra Leone had been exploited to build and sustain Western capitalism. This is true for many countries in Africa. At the dawn of British capitalism in 1783, which had been stimulated by slave labour in cotton and sugar plantations, Europe acknowledged the importance of slaves for the accomplishment of its new phenomenon of capitalism that had captured the interest and curiosity of its peoples. "In June 1783, the Prime Minister, Lord North, complimented the Quaker[2] opponents of the slave trade on their humanity, but regretted that its abolition was an impossibility, as the trade had become necessary to almost every nation in Europe. Slave traders and sugar planters rubbed their hands in glee."[3] This was contrary to Ottobah Cugoano[4] and Olaudah Equiano's[5] advocacy letters for the freed slaves in England and Africans in the continent.

Ottobah and Olaudah were freed slaves who had managed to read and write, "Both insisted that English industries would benefit if the slave trade ceased. Vassa (Olaudah Equiano) in his book and in a letter to the secretary of state suggested that treating Africans as customers, not merchandise, would bring manufacturers vast profit."[6] Ignatius Sancho, another freed slave's letter was the first published material in England in 1782 by a black man. It too advocated the same notion for the black man as Ottobah and Olaudah.

87

It was an oxymoron when the British sent the freed slaves to Sierra Leone, made them swear allegiance to the king, and yet called it the Province of Freedom. And thus, Sierra Leone inherited an edition of the British constitution that England designed for advancing economic imperialism into post-independent epoch in Sierra Leone.

On Independence Day, April 27, 1961, England gave Sierra Leone a flag in exchange of its huge foreign reserves in her banks. Now, with grave indifference to the root of the problem, the West blames everything on corruption and talks ill of Africans in general. Like all African countries, Sierra Leone had to catch up with the rising rate of world inflation with no economic foundation compounded by excessive corruption.

Africans must not be deceived by the much talked about corruption in Africa. The most sophisticated forms of corruption are up and running in Western nations. Just as African nations are apprentices to capitalism, so they are to everything else that comes in the entire package. Like Sierra Leone, many African countries are economic deserts, which is why they suffer the brunt of corruption more than their rich counterparts in Western nations do. One writer calls Africa an economic Bermuda Triangle—where money disappears as soon as it reaches there. Because by the time Western expatriates heading project implementation units (PIUs) are excessively paid on contracts and international banks siphoned most of the money back to the West through outrageous procurement cost of Western goods from Western companies, alongside African leaders lining their pockets with public funds at the tail end of the process, often left are starving populations in Africa.

Corruption in the West is well, up and running—is so severe that it is not limited to governments alone. Big corporations have designed foolproof methods to defraud government coffers in Western countries. From the medical industry to the service and manufacturing, all defraud billions and billions of dollars from taxpayers many a time in cohort with government officials. Big insurance companies and medical providers bill government billions and billions of dollars for services they do not provide or under provide especially on behalf of poor people. The Enron and Halliburton companies in the United States are examples of such actions. The recent financial malpractice in the handling of funds for Hurricane Katrina victims is another to name a couple.

In fact, poor people pay more taxes in some of these Western nations than rich people and big corporations do. The rich have a hundred-and-one ways of evading taxes, all neatly embedded in corruption. Politicians are always in fraudulence scandals related to big deals equal to or more than those deals that African leaders pull off that often end up bankrupting African economies. Now Pres. George Bush of the United States is chasing against time to transfer the social securities of poor people, especially minorities, into the hands of big businesses, who would make big profits from them and later file for bankruptcy under one of those bankruptcy protection chapters we discussed earlier. Senators in the United States have been investigated recently in what is described as the biggest scandal in Congress in over a century for big money deals with a shade American political lobbyist, Republican political activist and businessman, Jack Abramoff:

Members of Congress were included if they received over $10,000 from Abramoff, his clients or his partners and have allegedly done favors for Abramoff, his clients or his partners. Members who were acting on behalf of a constituent in their state were excluded, even if those constituents were Abramoff clients. Certain members who received less than $10,000 in Abramoff were included because of extensive allegations of favors done for Abramoff.[7]

"Street children phenomenon" in Africa is a product of colonialism and imperialist corruption that African leaders inherited. To find an African child on the street was a strange occurrence. The typical African children were on the farms with their parents, learning new methods of survival, improving on the farming, and hunting tools. But when colonial governments tortured, raped, jailed, and killed many African parents, it surely brought about the "street children phenomenon." For example, during Operation Anvil in Kenya, many natives, in the thousands, were arrested and "classified as 'white,' 'grey,' or 'black'"[8] to show who was most dangerous. In this colour-coding scheme, the colonial master considered those that were coded black as the most dangerous to society, where white being clean and not a threat to society. Grey dangled in between these two extremes as a pendulum, whose fate depended upon the colonial administrators' discretion. Even though all the prisoners were black, the colour-coding scheme was nothing but an object of racism, colonialism, and its traditional method of "divide and conquer."

The street children, thus, would look cool in the eyes of other children who would copy this new fad. Many of them these days just do not have a choice but to be on the street because of hardship. First, colonial masters and Western investors had stolen their monies, and now their own corrupt governments who have mastered the art of corruption so well from their former colonial masters have taken over the process. It is reported in the September 2005 "Africa: Whatever You Thought, Think Again" special edition *National Geographic* magazine that there are about 15,000 to 25,000 street children in Nairobi, Kenya. Although AIDS has been partly responsible for this hike, waywardness, which is due to poverty, remains the prime contributor. The same is true of many big cities in Africa. It is apparent that a country such as Sierra Leone would have "a pool of idle and disgruntled youth" to become ruthless partners in warfare.

Many times, Western investors help corrupt African leaders through bribery. They bribe authorities in Africa with huge sums of monies; they call it kickbacks, but also declare them into the cost of doing business, and they end up reporting nothing or little profits to the African governments to facilitate tax evasion. Also, colonial masters strangulated African economies by turning them into farming and mining economies in the business of producing raw material for big factories and manufacturing industries in Western nations. Today these same nations, now turned economic imperialists, encourage African nations to remain as farmers and miners to support their factories.

Manufacturing, but not farming economies alone, dominates the global market. Farming economies sometimes only survive for a short while as in Ivory Coast and Ghana in the past during the cacao boom. Now Ghana is set up for the same mistake once more. It is not embarking on a serious manufacturing sector while things are glossy until its bubble will bust once more, and the Ghanaians would stand in long lines once again to buy toothpaste as they did before.

The UN economic report on Africa 2005 states, "The share of the total population living below the $1 a day threshold of 46 per cent is higher today than in the 1980s and 1990s—this despite significant improvements in the growth of Africa GDP in recent years."[9] It reports the highest GDP growth of 4.6 percent average in about ten years. But when this figure is broken down into separate countries, the result becomes intriguing. Although most countries in Africa failed to meet the 7 percent or more Millennium Development Goal requirement, yet few countries have alarming figures. For example, Chad's GDP growth for 2005 is 39 percent, Equatorial Guinea for the same year is 18.3 percent and the surprising 15 percent for post-war Liberia. Oil boom certainly accounts for the hike in the GDP growth in Chad and Equatorial Guinea while that of Liberia's is definitely from post-war reconstruction aid. Other countries such as Ethiopia, Angola, and Mozambique exceeded the 7 percent GDP growth considerably. Nonetheless, their GDP hikes are consistent with mineral/aid contribution.

However, the revelation is that these colonial boundaries in Africa are no doubt poverty victims of the "divided we fall" maxim. Just as Nevada is not a barren land in the United States, so must there be no barren lands in Africa. Evidently, there is a significant GDP growth for Africa. On the other hand, majority of these countries insistence in the negative figures clearly is the effect of colonization and division of Africa. Thus, the UN economic report on Africa 2005's statement is clearly an oxymoron: how could there be an increase in growth of 4.6 percent over ten years and poverty at once? Africa must let go of these boundaries to consolidate in resources and maximize its capacity in the global market, not these folly recommendations from the G8 and other Western nations. Bottom-line, not many countries can boast of recording an average of 4.6 percent GDP over 10 years span. It simply means that the continent can only prosper as a nation.

Now the G8 nations have on their agenda, spearheaded by Britain, "debt relief" for African nations. The G8 includes the same nations who partitioned the great nations of Africa into small feeble countries in the late nineteen century, plundered them, brought them on their knees, and turned them into handicaps. This trend is consistent with what has happened in the past: slavery, colonialism, political and economic imperialism, and now debt relief, all cloaked in crooked intentions to enrich Western capitalist nations. This action by the G8 smells like another "Scramble for Africa" according to the investigative report by the Guardian newspaper:

A Guardian investigation beginning today reveals that instead of enriching often debt-ridden countries, some big corporations are accused by campaigners of facilitating corruption and provoking instability—so much so that organizations such as Friends of the Earth talk of an 'oil curse.'

Simon Taylor, director of Global Witness, which has been prominent in urging reform, said: 'Western companies and banks have colluded in stripping Africa's resources. We need to track revenues from oil, mining and logging into national budgets to make sure that the money isn't siphoned off by corrupt officials.'

Looting of state assets by corrupt leaders should become a crime under international law, he said. 'The G8 should take the lead in this.' The original Scramble for Africa took place in the late 19th century, when Britain, France and Germany competed to carve Africa into colonies. Today corporations from the US, France, Britain and China are competing to profit from the rulers of often chaotic and corrupt regimes. Our investigations in three African countries rich in resources—Angola, Equatorial Guinea and Liberia—show how British-based companies have negotiated deals that critics say are against the interests of some of the poorest and most traumatized people on earth. The Guardian's inquiries focus on a big gas project in Equatorial Guinea; plans to exploit Liberia's diamonds, and western banks' readiness to provide Angola with huge oil-backed loans. In Equatorial Guinea, BG plc. (formerly the British Gas state company) has closed a deal with the regime of President Teodoro Obiang to buy up the country's production of liquefied natural gas for the next 17 years. Britain's HSBC bank has been accused by a U.S. Senate committee of helping Mr. Obiang move cash from the country's oil revenues into financial 'black holes' in Luxembourg and Cyprus. The country is threatened with repeated coups by outsiders keen to get their hands on the oil wealth. In Liberia, which has been beset by civil war, LIB, a private London bank, was behind attempts to monopolise alluvial diamond production and the country's telecommunications. The UN and the World Bank have criticised the schemes as secretive and against the country's interests. LIB has now withdrawn. And in Angola, the victim of an even more destructive internal war, one of the UK's leading development banks, Standard Chartered, has been accused of damaging the country's economy by providing record multibillion dollar loans which give a stranglehold over future oil production. A succession of scandals has already revealed how oil wealth was looted in billions from the former Abacha military regime in Nigeria with the assistance of western banks and bribes paid by US oil firms. In Sudan and Chad, Chinese companies are moving in, backing and arming military rulers and building pipelines. And in France, the then state oil company Elf has been accused in corruption investigations of having paid kickbacks and encouraged regimes to run up debts as part of a deliberate 'African strategy.' Congo-Brazzaville, the fourth-largest sub-Saharan oil producer, was dominated by Elf, and now has the highest per capita debt in the world. Global Witness says in a 2004 report: 'Oil wealth [there] has left a legacy of corruption, poverty and conflict.'[10]

This is the complex forms of corruption these big Western capitalist investors would introduce in Africa where there are insufficient funds to go around corrupt officials and run governments at the same time.

That is how many Africans become refugees and economic immigrants in the West. Because of the wars European slave masters, colonialists, neo-colonialists, and economic imperialists caused. It makes commodious good sense for many Africans to live in the West in marginal-living conditions instead of going back to Africa.

The marginal living condition for Africans could just be a perception or more precisely a comparison to other non-Africans outside the continent. First, Western nations not only create the need for Africans to become economic wanderers in the world, but also over-scrutinized them through immigration changes of status process and discrimination, thereby stunting their personal growth in the process when stacked up against other non-African economic immigrants. People of European and of other light skin ancestries have had better chance of resettlement in Western countries compared to Africans. Even the descendants of Africans who were taken hundreds of years ago through slavery are still being marginalized in the United States, Canada, England, and many other European nations.

Let us examine the West's interests in the Middle East; it could not be just for oil. Besides oil, the entire Middle East sits between Washington and Moscow politically. It was a strategic position of interest to the Pentagon more than it was for the Department of Commerce or State Department at the height of the cold war. But let us suggest for a minute the Middle East's relation with the West is for economic interest. The West has been plundering Africa over five hundred years and still cares less about the advancement of its peoples. Therefore, economic interest could not be a compelling reason for the West to pay attention to any region on which they have clamped massive imperial mandibles.

Thus, the United States was not just interested in drilling oil in the Middle East even though oil was/is of great interest to its economy. But now that the cold war had been put to rest, the war of terrorism has become the next important reason to advance the relationship between the Middle East and Western relations.

Besides North Africa, which is also of concern in the War of Terror, military bases in Africa are useless. Even the one in Liberia was of no use anymore after conventional warfare had been replaced by long-range missiles and high-tech warfare, which explains partly why the United States looked on as Liberians slaughtered each other. The reason for this is that Africa is so far away from missile range to Moscow it has no military interest to the United States and the rest of Western nations. Also, apart from North Africa, which is already in Western radars, Africa has no business in terrorist activities except that terrorists have taken advantage of its vulnerability to camp and strike at Western interests as in the August 7, 1998, bombings of the United States embassies in Nairobi and Dar es Salaam, and the dirty blood diamond trade in Sierra Leone's civil war that has been associated with source of income for Al-Qaida.

The West had accomplished its political and economic agenda in Africa when communism fell. Just imagine how much confidence communism could have mustered from these many African nations, their raw material and peoples. Indeed, Moscow strongly believed that a victory in the third world was a victory in the cold war. This is the suggestion Andrew and Mitrokhin echo in their most authoritative account of the cold war: *The World Was Going Our Way: the KGB and the Battle for the Third World.*

This partly explains why Western nations seldom help Africans through resettlement programs unlike other individuals and groups of Caucasian race and other people from other light skin ancestries. Doing so does not make any statement of political interest. On the other hand, Western governments assist such groups and transform them into political pressure groups to hear their voices against their oppressors. Many a time, especially the U.S. government, organizes them as subversive groups, arms them, finances them—in the name of democracy—and sends them off to fight against their oppressive governments. Cubans, Iraqis, Chinese, North Vietnamese, North Koreans, many more Caucasian, Asian, and light skin peoples' dissidents are examples. At the end of the day, the United States benefits from a mushroom of military bases all over the world and sometimes imposes political ideology in these pseudo-colonies. Meanwhile, once these people settle, they enjoy a better social standard than even the African American who was the first Negro, the Negro who preceded the steam engine, the Negro whose blood, sweat, muscles, and bones were the coal and crankshaft of Western industrialization. Simply, what chance has the second Negro has for resettlement and protection against violations of his fundamental human rights in Western nations in a true sense of the act?

Meanwhile on the continent of Africa, these partitioned nations bear the heaviest burden of the refugee crisis that is caused by Western facilitated and sponsored wars. Yet the Western media highlight few individuals, few families or small groups of refugees who are sponsored by private people or NGOs to travel abroad, taking credit for helping, punctuated with the good old "When One Person Can Make a Difference—'One Starfish'" allegory. It is extremely illogical that they, however, at the same time show throng of refugees on the TV, in camps in Africa, in destitution, and in mockery of their plight as in the Darfur region of Sudan.

For the rest of the world, it makes sense that these Western humanitarian organizations would choose to highlight few well-cared-for groups as subjects of propaganda to attract more international funding. Meanwhile, multitudes of refugees languish in the countries whose economies had been strangulated because their leaders were busy side-taking in the spheres of ideological, political and financial influence amongst Western nations and creating internecine rivalry that would become the naissance of these many "civil wars." These are the wars that are causing the refugee crisis in the first place—aftermath of the cold war and the struggle over spoils of war. Yet these few highlighted groups get part of donor monies with the majority going into administrative cost and unreasonable executives' salaries. Read on what has been recently published on refugee, hunger, and starvation in Africa.

According to aid agencies, a vast "hunger belt" stretches across the Sahel region from Mauritania, Burkina Faso and Mali in west Africa through Niger and Chad in central Africa, to Sudan, Ethiopia, Eritrea, and reaching as far as Somalia on the Indian Ocean coast. The US-funded Famine Early Warning System Network (FEWS Net), which brings together aid agencies active in Africa, estimates that more than 20 million people in at least seven countries are facing "food emergencies."

Recently, media attention has focused on the hunger crisis in Niger where some 3.6 million of the country's 11.5 million people are hungry due to drought and locust plagues last year. More than 2.5 million people are described by the World Food Program as being "extremely vulnerable and in need of food assistance," including 800,000 children. There are fears that 150,000 kids could starve to death before October.

Yet this unfolding humanitarian disaster was studiously ignored by the leaders of the world's richest countries meeting in Scotland on July 6–8 where they supposedly proclaimed a "new deal" between the rich countries and the poor in Africa. Nor did the world's capitalist media—which was busy lauding the Group of Eight industrialized countries' "historic" plan to conditionally cancel multilateral debts owed by a few African countries as the dawning of a new era of international social justice—interrupt the hype to note that millions of Africans were starving at that very moment due to the G8 governments' miserliness and their imposition of free-market policies.

It was only when a BBC reporter and camera crew emerged from Niger in mid-July with shocking footage of starving children, threatening to expose the G8's massive hypocrisy and cynicism that Western governments reluctantly increased aid to Niger from virtually zero to an inadequate trickle.

It soon emerged that the UN had first issued an alert in November warning that the poor of Niger faced severe hunger and called for Western governments to fund aid. Next to nothing arrived. In March, another appeal for $16 million resulted in a meagre $1 million. A May 25 call for $30 million again resulted in little. It was repeated on July 8 and only resulted in $10 million, the vast bulk of that only coming in after the BBC aired its report. On August 5, the

UN announced that $80 million was now required to make up for the tardiness in responding to its earlier calls.[11]

Meanwhile, the West hurries to these troubled spots in Africa to seek their economic interest only, throwing their weights around anything in power to stay in business. In Sierra Leone, during the decade-long rebel war, a United States corporation signed a lease with rebel leaders to mine the Tongo Field kimberlite dike for diamonds. "Omrie Golley had earlier in the year courted me on behalf of a Canadian company concerning the No. 19 tailings site that aborts the kimberlite dikes in Tongo Field that an American company and mine had leased from the National Provisional Ruling Council (NPRC) in February 1994."[12]

In 2001, a handful of refugees were brought to the United States from Sierra Leone by Friends of Sierra Leone.[13] The group organized a fund-raiser dubbed Gift of Limbs' celebrity picnic in collaboration that raised $45,000 to help defray expenses.[14] First, to sensationalize the fund-raiser they referred to the refugees as Sierra Leonean amputees. In their literature, not in the sense of their present amputated condition, but that the rebels amputated them. For goodness sake, machete-wielding rebels in a conflict that originated in Liberia hacked off these people's limbs. Interestingly, its origin could be traced back to the bad resettlement process of slaves in Monrovia by the American Colonization Society. The sponsors of the fund-raiser failed to realize that people perform amputation only for medical reasons unlike what happened in Sierra Leone to thousands of war victims.

Nonetheless, the occasion was well attended. Former President Clinton and Senator Hillary Clinton were in attendance and many more celebrities. They raised hundreds of thousands of dollars for few refugees, which was good. My daughter, Fatima Kabba, still adores the teddy bear Bill Clinton autographed for her for her $5.00 entrance fee per child.

But if these people were here under family or organization sponsorship, would it not make sense that they use their presence to raise money for the hundreds of thousands languishing in destitute camps in Africa? Whose greatest daily accomplishments have been reduced to a cup of clean water and a meal? Those are the refugees always in dire need of help, and the opportune ones once here, it makes commodious good sense for them to serve as good faith ambassadors for the larger problem, raise funds, and draw the attention of philanthropists and international aid organizations to the crisis in these many camps in Africa.

Repeatedly, Africans have been marginalized. Recently, the UN organ responsible for crisis funds for the recent tsunami victims, in response to excess funding, shamelessly announced on a TV broadcast that donors must stop contributing to funds when they have no funds allocation for refugees in Western Sudan in Darfur region. Even where there is a surplus, they would prefer to dump it than to helping Africa. How could the UN not take advantage of such response to crisis in one region to help another region? In fact, those who have no connection or special interest in Africa, just from watching or listening to the news, did not know the Tsunami affected East Africa as well nonetheless the crimes against humanity in the killing fields of Darfur, which the UN still falls short of calling a crime of genocide.

The media shy away from addressing such issues in a positive way that would help Africa. They are only interested in sensationalizing crisis in Africa, but not in resolving them. You should have seen the race to report the Ebola virus outbreak in DR Congo. They had many journalists in those villages to show the faces of the dying people on TV news than they had health service workers to help the living.

That is the plight of Africans both in Africa and outside of Africa. One could rationalize Africa's underperformance to other secondary factors compounded by primary factors, such as slavery, colonialism, imperialism, and now racism and discrimination. Coming to acceptance with living in the

West for Africans is turning out to be more meaningful than dodging bullets and rebel advances in many African countries. It is a lesser of two evils, so to speak. However, an innate human tendency to live as equal tends to make Africans measure their living standard expectation to not what awaits them in Africa, but to that of the western countries they reside. The thing that Africa is still struggling to grasp with, amid this state of confusion, is that canon concept that would make Africa look, even in the eyes of African Americans, as the promised land to willingly return to away from racism and discrimination, the land that will develop Africans' disposition to the rest of the world as equals—tourists and businessmen or women—not as political or economic refugees.

CHAPTER NINE

The Revolution

Naturally, Africa is a communal society. Also the law of nature prevails in the state of nature where lies perfect liberty that is different from the limited democracy of modern societies. No society is perfect in a form in which absolute liberty thrives. For tyranny easily flourishes alongside absolute liberty, in which the strongest reigns in a system of survival of the fittest. Thus, in a state of nature, absolute liberty and tyranny thrive alongside each other.

Up to the twenty-first century, Africa seems to be, for the most part, in its natural form. Africa is yet to develop into a strong socioeconomic society capable of taking it completely out of its natural form. Capitalism and communism only sunk Africa deeper. For the sprouting despotic regimes in Africa, in the aftermath of the cold war, apparently, are far worse than the continent in its state of nature. For many, thriving societies borrowed ideas from everywhere and tailored them to their cultures and traditions to form strong civil societies. Unlike nearly every nation that has been branded as a third world nation in the world is lacking an original ideal or is copycatting one of the following: capitalism or communism.

Africa by far is the most economically suitable human habitat today; the continent has not changed very much. This is not a known fact to Africans alone; Wayne Madsen wrote of Bill Clinton's foreign affairs committee chairman, Lee Hamilton, saying, "Africa has the most economic potential of any region in the world."[cxvi] For these reasons, Africa has attracted many different peoples at different times. Sharp contrast between the face of North Africa and black Africa is a result of early immigration into Africa from the Middle East, Asia, and Europe. The Boers once in South Africa saw the need to stay there and make it a home. Some of the reasons behind this are very basic (non-scientific) in nature. The climatic condition in Africa is so suitable for human habitation that the snowploughs that the former Soviet Union shipped to Ethiopia were never put to use. The financial effect of nature, say snow alone, every year on Western nations totals in the billions of dollars.

That is why Arab people occupied the whole of North Africa, and why many slave traders stayed behind. Colonialists as well, such as the greatest selfish thinker of all times, Ian Smith in the Rhodesia, became settlers all around Africa. Dutch, Germans, Portuguese, British, and Spanish went to Africa in large numbers and stayed. The climate is good, the land is arable, and the African peoples are receptive and warm.

The condition above prepared Africa with a rich and diversified culture, which was rendered useless for progress because of slavery and colonialism. But a mixture of these people's rich cultures and religious traditions is what Africa needs to take full advantage of now. A blend of African traditionalism with these various cultures could have become the most diversified society and most powerful continent in the world.

It suffices to note that communalism economic system in ancient Africa was nothing one could compare to ancient and medieval European communal societies. The ancient black man built "African communalism" on solid economic concepts and theories that were in progress before Africa was derailed by Arabs and Europeans into slavery and later the state of absolutism. Entirely, it was unlike Lower and Upper Palaeolithic hunter-gatherer societies of Europe. The latter were mere scavenging, hunting, and gathering for families and communities sustenance.

When a British philanthropist Granville Sharp, upon establishing the Province of Freedom in Sierra Leone, wrote these words, "Every ten householders would form a tithing, every ten tithings a hundred, collectively responsible for preserving order and keeping watch against outside enemies, each householder with a voice in a Common Council,"[cxvii] as a recommendation for a tentative constitution for the repatriated African in Sierra Leone, he had made a good observation of the Africans. Secondly, he had envisioned Europeans would return to enslave Africans on their own land.

No wonder Europeans had perceived Africa was moving toward feudalism when it was wedged between African communalism and capitalism at one time. Capitalism was entirely an alien economic system, which Europeans had brought to Africa. It has turned out to be undesirable to its culture and tradition.

It seems that ancient Africans were somewhat sceptical to join the bandwagon of ruthless use of human resources to create a surplus of everything for the few powerful people in their societies. Thus, Africa was stuck between these two economic systems. It seems like the limbo of disdain for capitalism that causes the reluctance in Africans to adopt capitalism wholesomely. Apparently, post-independent African leaders leaned more toward communism because it was confused with African communalism. The absence of a natural economic system in Africa is equal to a socioeconomic and geopolitical stagnation or degradation.

European historians would observe this economic state of stagnation and confusion wrongly and asserted it was a feudal system in the early days of Africa's relation with Europe. Naturally, feudalism is the transition to capitalism and dangling between these two entirely different systems—

African communalism and European capitalism—would sure look like feudalism.

The fact of the matter is Western capitalism swept a confused Africa off its feet and brought it on its knees. African societies were progressive when their economic ideal was African communalism, a complex system, which was based on market economy before the advent of Western capitalist and Eastern communism systems. African communalism's horizon was the families as the smallest units of its societies within nation-states.

The claim that Africa is the richest in human resources cannot be an empty assertion lest Europeans would have found the slave trade unprofitable. They would have abandoned it voluntarily long before they did. This is evident in Africans' resilience against Europeans' smallpox and slaving that had almost wiped out the Indian population in the New World. And to this day, Africans have continued to manifest superior leadership in academia, music and the arts, entertainment and sports worldwide.

It means that Africa's wealth of human resources is not only quantitative, but also qualitative. There is no need to discuss Africa's size and riches in natural resources. What we need to discuss, as we have already done, is how Africa has been exploited and continues to be exploited by foreigners. But above all, we must also discuss how we can pull these individual languages, cultures and traditions, separate nationalities, and the Diaspora talents and resources together for a progressive African communal society. The simple reason is that human and natural resources exploitation by imperialists have made Africa so vulnerable that one can only measure its wealth in terms of that of its exploiters.

We must turn our families and communities into bigger African communalists that can match the productive powers of Western capitalists. By no means must we confuse families and communities' communalism of Africa with individual capitalists of the West or state ownership communism of the East. Africans had great desire for massive accumulation of wealth as well. And Africans always loathed state ownership of its wealth. "After making a tour of the city, Leo Africanus wrote, 'Here are a great store of doctors, judges, priests, and other learned men that are bountifully maintained at the king's cost and charges. And hither are brought diverse books, which are sold for more money than any other merchandise.' He was surprised at the wealth of the people and envied their many wells 'containing most sweet water.'"[cxviii] Many other studies have also supported that market economy had existed in Africa before Western capitalism. One notable work is that of Elias N. Saad. In his award-winning doctoral dissertation *Social History of Timbuktu, 1400-1900: The Role of Muslim Scholars and Notables*, he wrote,

At the level of economics, similar considerations went into operation. Timbuktu, like other commercial centres, benefited immensely from the regularity and safety of trade brought about by the exigencies of the empire-building. The rulers, for their part, had no interest in directly controlling these centres so long as a laissez-fairs policy secured the flow of goods to and from their domains.

There was no question, here as elsewhere outside the Western world, of the city evolving a corporate character with a legally defined body of citizenry. A rudimentary tendency in that direction is evidenced in the case of Jenne, Timbuktu's major trade partner to the south, judging from the legends which recall that city-state's Islamization. But the need for encouraging the arrival of merchants, whether for short or extended stay or permanent settlement, reinforced the ad hoc character of urban organization.[cxix]

The freedom to accumulate wealth is a fundamental principle for a progressive society. But how must Africa tailor this concept to fit the nature of its families and communities? By nature, Africans share everything with families and extended families. This nature has been a contributing factor for corruption in Africa in the first place. Many Africans holding positions in politics or in management or even in the private sector, for the most part, equally make extended families' problems their problems. This is how sensitive government positions are filled with "square pegs in round holes," the need to satisfy family and extended family members whom go unquestioned for tardiness, corruption, and or incompetence. Unconsciously, many African governments become predominantly filled with robbers who rob government coffers to meet the needs of large and extended families.

Thus, if such is the nature of African people, then Africa has failed by copycatting capitalism or communism, which have individualism and state ownership as prerequisites for their success or failure respectively. These are two extremes that have proven not fit for Africa and its peoples. It seems then that for this reason, African ancestry long before Europeans focused on the family as the smallest unit of their societies to build strong communities.

In Timbuktu, "up until the French colonial period, family councils called qadis handled even serious crimes, such as murder and robbery."[cxx] Up to present-day Africa, families, extended families, and communities are the owners and runners of many successful businesses. Somehow, through African communalism, Africa must explore how it can focus on the family to minimize corruption in the first place and reduce brain drain from the continent.

The United Nation's International Labour Organization figures indicate that about 2 percent of the African population is international migrant, and that 10 percent will become international migrant, all things remaining equal, by 2015.[cxxi] And we are witnessing a new trend that some Western nations have made basic education a criterion to issue travelling visa lately. It means that Europeans are demanding to have only the best Africans immigrate to their countries thereby aggravating the brain drain in the continent.

Exploitation is the reason behind the serious problem of brain drain in Africa in the epochs of slavery, colonialism, and imperialism. And it is why many Africans find themselves in the West. This work is an inquiry into the avaricious obliteration of the wealth of Africa and its social effect on the fabric of the African society.

The goal is a sweet pill for a United African States (UAS) and people with a clear national consciousness. It is a tough call, but with an understanding that like every tough call, especially a controversial one as this may be, always brings two things—prominence or harsh criticism. But before we do that, we must tread cautiously to avoid further disruptions of societies by heeding to Socrates' admonishment:

And will you, O professor of true virtue, say that you are justified in this? Has a philosopher like you failed to discover that our country is more to be valued and higher and holier far than mother or father or any ancestor, and more to be regarded in the eyes of the gods and of men of understanding? also to be soothed, and gently and reverently entreated when angry, even more than a father, and if not persuaded, obeyed? And when we are punished by her, whether with imprisonment or stripes, the punishment is to be endured in silence; and if she leads us to wounds or death in battle, thither we follow as is right; neither may anyone yield or retreat or leave his rank, but whether in battle or in a court of law, or in any other place, he must do what his city and his country order him; or he must change their view of what is just: and if he may do no violence to his father or mother, much less may he do violence to his country. What answer shall we make to this, Crito? Do the laws speak truly, or do they not?[cxxii]

We must also now examine fable Timbuktu before we envision our modern Timbuktu of under African communalism:

Fabled Timbuktu clings to the edge of the Sahara Desert. The city lies in the Sahel (the southern edge of the Sahara), eight miles north of the Niger River in the West African nation of Mali. Two-story mud-brick houses crowd narrow streets filled with ankle-deep sand. Only a few structures—a couple of hotels and the minarets of old mosques (Islamic houses of prayer)—rise into the pale blue sky. A visitor can walk from one end of Timbuktu to the other in less than 20 minutes. The city's small population of just over 20,000 come from a rich ethnic background that has both Arab and black African roots.

Four Hundred years ago, however, Timbuktu was a thriving metropolis of more than 100,000 people, with two universities, 180 schools, and more than 20,000 scholars. From a small campground along the banks of the Niger River, Timbuktu had grown to become known as the 'Pearl of Africa.'[cxxiii]

"Economic development will work miracle in Timbuktu. All we need is some peace." And the following is my vision of a new Timbuktu: a solid democratic society for all Africa. A Timbuktu of a solid polity whose peoples must be equipped with what Robert A. Dahl, an emeritus professor at Yale University, one of the world's best-known political scientists, refers to as "civic competence."[cxxiv] But while borrowing from highly competent political experts and great political systems, we must not think, once again, that there is no alternative to international communism and capitalism.

These have been the greatest enemy of Africa and Timbuktu. These are the makers of the Timbuktu of Larry Brook's description. But we are done discussing all that. Now we must discuss the Africa and the Timbuktu of our envisioning. When Professor Dahl wrote the following words, he was not referring to communism, socialism, or capitalism. Instead, he was only bringing to our consciousness one of the essential ingredients of a solid democracy:

If democracy were to work, it would seem to require a certain level of political competence on the part of its citizens. In newly democratic or democratizing countries, where people are just beginning to learn the arts of self-government, the question of citizen competence possesses an obvious urgency. Yet even in countries where democratic institutions have existed for several generations or more, a growing body of evidence reveals grave limits to citizen competence. These limits are serious enough to require a systematic search for new ways of enhancing civic competence, several of which I will discuss below. Should these prove feasible, they could be employed to improve citizen competence not only in the older democracies but also in fledging democratic countries where the problem may be even acute.[cxxv]

Many events of the past to the present have robbed Africa of this very critical element of a good polity in several ways I have discussed throughout this work. Slavery, colonialism, economic and political imperialism have all stolen from African peoples their civic competence to form a polity that is not insensitive to their way of life. Africa was so divided by the colonialists' divide-and-conquer phenomenon that there were few "trustworthy surrogates"[cxxvi] among its people in post-independence era. Africans were busy undermining each other for various reasons: communism versus capitalism, nationalists versus colonialists' stooges, and so on. The African citizenry was so polarized that "trusted surrogates" were not necessarily "trustworthy surrogates." They could be easily bought and sold by different factions of the era. It was this culture of betrayal, which would become an attribute of being an African politician in post-independent Africa. It greatly undermined all political institutions in Africa by derailing the peoples' attention from creativity in favour of adoption of foreign political and economic systems, thereby warring against each other on behalf of international political ideologues who would turn round and called it tribal and ethnic wars.

Adoption of foreign political and economic systems that are unsympathetic to African peoples, their cultures and traditions after independence, fostered civil wars, economic imperialism, unsustainable economies, and incompetent civic citizenry. Simply, that is the disease African nations are suffering from.

But the constant good old moaning and groaning of the past must stop. We must swallow this single dose prescription in this work and become creative again. There is no substitute to a thinking-hat if this trend of economic, social, and political backwardness must change to innovative and forward-looking economic, social, and political African Society. Let us reflect once more on my favourite rhetorical flourish by Johnnie Cochran: "If it doesn't fit, you must acquit."

What is not new in Africa is self-governance. Africa's great kingdoms, like other nations, have been governing themselves well way before the interruption of the trend by foreign infiltrations. It suffices to say that hunger and starvation are the new problems in Africa if we compare ancient times to modern Africa. The immediate example is the sharp contrast between Timbuktu before the advent of Europeans and the Timbuktu today. What is more, the only time we can come close to comparing Africa and Europe is to compare their ancient epochs. It is only then, taking into account then and now, we must agree that, to be reasonable, Europe was not too far advanced than Timbuktu. But the sharp contrast today between Europe and Timbuktu is as daylight and night. Evidently, the slave masters took healthy Africans; in fact, every African the slave masters took was very healthy. It means that starvation was not a known phenomenon. Thus, the black man must have been doing something right in his own ways before the disruption of his way of life.

As early as the seventeenth-century, monarchs ruled many European nations and so was Africa. What Africa was deprived off was a smooth transition from kingdoms to representative democracies and the construction of civil societies as we see them today. Every change was sudden and abrupt—kingdoms were torn apart, and kings were turned into slave hunters; kingdoms were broken into colonies without the peoples' consent, and colonies were turned into economic empires. In essence, it was not the people that rose against absolutism. In which case, the people would have had alternatives to their monarchs.

As if slavery and colonialism were nothing, the cold war turned African leaders into tyrants, mass murderers, despots, autocrats, aristocrats, military dictators, rebels, anything but democrats and civil and law abiding citizens. Military rules and/or one-party systems popped up across the hills and valleys of Africa like a bag of popcorn in a hot oven.

African leaders, many in their graves, will answer, "Yeah!" one way or another to the KGB or the CIA. Adding more reasons why Africa must go back to what it was doing right when it kept healthy people roaming its hills and valleys, its savannah and forestland (Timbuk-Traditionalism—political system and African communalism—economic ideal).

There is no time better than today now that Africa has been enriched with a wealth of great cultures, traditions, and religions of the world through slavery, colonialism, and economic imperialism. The greatest civilization today anyone can envision in the world would be an African civilization that only needs to severe its dependency on international communism, socialism, and capitalism. When Africa borrows great aspects of these great cultures around the world, the following will emerge—Timbuk-Traditionalist-Islamic-Judeo-Christian African civilization on an economic track of African communalism ideals that would include the whole Africa. The good old saying "Divided we fall, united we stand" is not a rocket science maxim.

Communism and capitalism are two extremes: the state and the individual. And they have claimed that there is a gap between communism and capitalism. But we have come back after five hundred years to tell them that there is a bridge there—the family. The family is supposed to be watching the building of a strong community with one eye and watching the development of the individual with the other eye. For this reason, the family is the ideal unit of a good polity. African peoples have been victims of foreign political systems for centuries. They must now rise up as one—black Africans, Arabs, Caucasians, Asians, and Spaniards. All to rise up as one people to bring their resources together, their cultures together, their traditions together, their religions together, and their political ideals together under African communalism and focus on the family as the smallest unit toward building a strong community of peoples.

Once accomplished, Timbuktu will be at her highest glory that one would imagine of a city of such fame and glory of the past. [cxxvii]

113

1000 AD, **7**

130-year-old Americo Liberian
Empire, **41**

17th century, **10**

500–400 BC, **7**

A Dialogue with History, **1**

a sunny land for shady people, **17**

a young Portuguese explorer who
discovered Sierra Leone, **20**

Abd al-Rahman al-Tamimi, **26**

ACDL (Association for Constitutional
Democracy in Liberia, **41**

Africa, **5, 7, 8, 9, 10, 11, 12, 13, 14,
15, 16, 17, 18, 19, 21, 37, 40, 43,
44,** *81,* **102, 103,** *104,*

Africa odyssey, **7**

African, **1, 7, 10, 11, 12, 13, 14, 15,
16, 18, 19, 24, 25, 27, 41, 42, 43,**
120

African American missionary, **16**

African communalism, **12, 15, 104,
105, 113**

African communalist societies, **15**

African peoples, **7**

African scholarship and philosophy,
10

African was ruled by a Mansa, **11**

African way of life, **12**

Africanist historians, **7**

Africans, **7, 8, 13, 14, 15, 16, 17, 18,
19, 22, 24, 44, 47, 48, 54, 55, 56,
57, 58, 59, 60, 61, 63, 64, 65, 69,
70, 71, 72, 73, 77, 84, 85, 87, 88,
94, 96, 98, 100, 102, 104, 105,
106, 107, 110, 111, 113**

al-maghrib, **10**

alphas, **25**

Al-sa'di, **10**

Al-Sadi, **9**

Al-Saᶜdiʰs TaᎯrīk al-sūdān, **26, 27**

America, **14, 19, 38, 45, 55, 82**

American Colonization Society, **37,
38, 39, 40, 42, 99**

Americas, **19**

And Leo Africanus, **8**

Arab, **10, 14, 31, 33, 36, 103, 109**

Arab al-maghrib, **10**

Arab scholars, **14**

aristocracy, **12, 74**

Aristotle, **13**

Askia Muhammad, **10**

Athens, **4, 11**

Australia, **19**

Australia and the Americas, **19**

Baring, **17, 120**

battle of East and West Europe, *45*

Belgian
Belgium, **17**

Bible, **7**

Britain, **17, 37, 38, 46, 92, 93**

British, **17, 37, 38**

British justice, **17**

capitalism, **1, 2, 15, 46, 51, 52, 72,
75, 87, 88, 102, 104, 106, 107,
109, 110, 112**

caravan of slaves across the Sahara or
a boatload of slaves across the
Atlantic, **12**

Charles Taylor, **41**

Cheikh Anta Diop, **8, 27, 120**

Christianity
Christian, **1, 10, 25**

Cicero, **12**

city-states, **8, 9**

colonialism, **7, 11, 15, 21, 22, 44, 45,**

52, 54, 55, 57, 69, 72, 75, 85, 86,
87, 90, 92, 100, 103, 107, 110,
112
colonialism manipulated and
distorted, 7
communism, 2, 12, 15, 47, 48, 51,
72, 73, 75, 96, 102, 104, 105,
107, 109, 110, 112
communism, socialism, or capitalism,
12, 109
Congo, 16, 17, 40, 70, 81, 82, 83
could have become the Timbuk-
Traditionalist-Islamic-Judeo-
Christian African civilization, 11
crimes of genocide perpetrated by
Europeans, 14
Daniel Webster, 38
dark continent, 7
David Anderson, 18
democracy, 12, 40, 41, 73, 74, 75,
76, 80, 81, 84, 96, 102, 109
Dia, 10, 24
Dia., 10
Dogon, 9
Dr. Patrick Seyon, 41
early wanderers at sea, 15
Egypt, 7, 8, 27
Egyptian civilization, 8
Egyptology, 9
Elias N. Saad, 10, 106
Emergency Committee, 17
Europeans, 7, 8, 14, 15, 16, 17, 18,
19, 39
extraction of iron, 7
extraordinarily sophisticated
cosmology, 9
family as the smallest unit of its
society, 15
Farma, 11
Farma (nu), 11

Fire from Timbuktu, 1, 2
Francis Afonso Dennis, 41
Francis Scott Key, 38
free-market economy, 15
Fulanis, 24
fweyeh, 35
fweyehnu, 35
Gao, 10
Gen. Thomas Quiwonkpa, 43
General Assembly in the autumn, *51*
General Erskine, 17
Germans, 18, 103
Ghadamis, 24
Ghana, 1
Githunguri, 17
global wars of conquest, 7
God Most High, 9
Great kingdoms existed in all Africa,
7
great religious reprimand, 7
Greco-Judeo-Christian Western
civilization, 1, 10
Greco-Roman, 8, 9
Greco-Roman civilization, 8
Greek philosophers, 9, 11
Greeks, 8
Greeks and Romans, 8
harram, 28
Henry Clay, 38
history on discovery, 7
Howard W. French, 9, 39
If it doesn't fit, you must acquit
Johnnie Cochran, 19, 111, 120
IHOP restaurant chain has on its all-
day American breakfast menu, pigs
in a blanket, 19
ill-gotten wealth, 8
imams, 25
imperialism, segregation, and
apartheid

imperialism
   segregation
      apartheid, 15
Imperialist rhetoric, 7
in-growing civilization in ancient
   Africa, 8
J. D. Fage, 8
J. Michael Fay, 7
Jenne, 8, 9, 10, 27, 28
Jenne-Jeno, 8
Jenne-Jeno and Timbuktu, 9
John Hunwick, 26
Johnnie Cochran, 19
John-Peter, *81*
Judaism, 10, 25
Jurists
   Jurist, 11
Kaba, 25, 27
Kabara, 24, 27, 28
Kabari, 24, 25, 26, 27
Kabba, 25, 99
karamohs, 25
Kenya, 17, 18
Khaba, 25
kiboko, 18
Kikuyu, 17
Kikuyu to the gallows, 17
King Leopold II
   King Leopold, 17, 18
kingship, 11, 12
kingship, aristocracy, and democracy,
   12
Kittles, *56*
Koi, 11
Kono, 27, 28, 30, 31, 32, 33, 34, 35,
   36
Koran, 7, 29
Krahn, 40
Kuba, 16

Kwame Nkrumah, 51
Liberia, 14, 17, 37, 38, 39, 40, 41,
   42, 43, *81*
Lion Mountain, 20
London, 120
Lord's Prayer, 13
lower and upper houses of legislation,
   11
Magsharen, 24
Mali, 1, 7, 8, 9, 13, 24, 27, 29
Malinke, 25
Mande-speaking people, 25
Mansa, 11
Master Sergeant Samuel Kanyon Doe,
   40
Mau Mau, 17, 18
Mau Mau rebellion, 18
megaflyover, 7
Middle East, 14
Mondyo, 11
Morocco, 10
Mossi, 9
mu'adhdhin, 25
Muhammad Muaddab al-kabari, 26
Muhammad Nad, 26
mujaddid, 25
mujtahid, 25
Nairobi, 18
Nairobi courthouse, 18
Negro, 8, 59, 96
Niger, 7, 27
Nigeria, 7, 41, 84
offshore slavery, 15
Pasha Mahmud b. Zargun, 9
peninsular mountain ranges, 20
People's Redemption Council (PRC),
   41
Peyima, 28

Politics, 9, 13
qadi, 26
removing Africans from mainland
    America, 14
revisionist history, 1
rickshaw boys, 18
road to civilization, 8
roaring of lions, 20
Romans, 8
Sahara, 12, 13, 14
Sahelo-sudanic west, 10
Samuel Doe, 41
Sanhaja Berber, 25
Sanhaja Berbers, 24
Senator John Tyler, 38
Shinjit, 26
Sierra Leone, 14, 24, 26, 27, 37, 38,
    41
Sirius, 9
Sirius, which at 8.6 light-years away is
    the brightest star in the sky, 9
SLBC, 20
socialism, 1, 12, 72, 109, 112
Songhai, 1, 8, 9, 10, 24, 25, 26, 27,
    29
St. Augustine (AD 354–430), 13
sultan of Mossi, 9
Sunni Ali, 9, 24, 26
Tadmekka, 10, 24
Tarikh al-Fattash, 10
The City of God, 13
The Republic and The Law, 12
These great stalwart men and women,
    who have from time immemorial
    been free, cultivating large farms
    of Indian corn, peas, tobacco,
    potatoes, trapping elephants for
    their ivory tusks and leopards for
    their skins, who have always had
    their own king and a government
not to be despised, officers of the
    law established in every town of
    the kingdom, these magnificent
    people, perhaps about 400,000 in
    number, have entered a new
    chapter in the history of tribe.
    Only a few years ago, travellers
    through here this country found
    them living in large homes, having
    from one to four rooms in each
    house, loving and living happily
    with their wives and children, one
    of the most prosperous and
    intelligent of all the African tribes .
    . ., 16
Timbuk-Traditionalism, 25, 31, 112
Timbuk-Traditionalist-Islamic
    African, 25
Timbuk-Traditionalist-Islamic-African
    civilization, 10
Timbuktu, 1, 8, 9, 10, 111
Timbuktu has been sacked three
    times, 9
Timbuktu Koy, 25
Timbuktu partly inherited its Islamic
    legacy from the south, 10
Tindirma, 10
trans-Sahara and trans-Atlantic slave
    trades
    trans-Sahara
        trans-Atlantic
            slave trade, 13
trans-Saharan slave trade, 14
Tuareg, 24
ulamas, 25
Walata, 24, 26, 27
Wangara, 24
Washington, 41, 42, 43, *81, 120*
West Africa, 7
Western capitalist cloak for plunder,
    17

Western civilization, 13, 17, 57

Western explorers, 12

Western Sudan, 8, 9

William Sheppard, 16

William Tolbert, 41, 42, 43

Yatah, 35

Yatanu, 35

Zagha, 10

[1] Samuel **Butler**, *Homer: The Iliad & The Odyssey*, (translated) (New York: Barnes & Nobles Books Publisher, 1999), 36.

[1] June 8, 2004: Biologist J. Michael Fay lifts off from Pretoria, South Africa, in a modification Cessna 182 . . . with a pilot, cameras, computerized maps, a global positioning system—and a will of steel. Flying low and slow over the continent's diverse ecosystems . . ., he compiled a visual record of Africa's environment from the most densely packed places to the wildest. Six months, ten thousand gallons of gas, and twenty-one countries later, Fay touched down in Portugal with more that twenty-nine thousand photographs . . . and a laptop full of data—hard-won material he hopes will inspire a long-term plan to preserve Africa's natural riches.

[1] David **Quammen**, "Tracing the Human Footprint," in the journal of *National Geographic*, Special Edition, *Africa: Whatever you Thought, Think Again*, September 2005 (Washington DC.: National Geographic, 2005), 21.

[2] David **Quammen**, "Tracing the Human Footprint," in the journal of *National Geographic*, Special Edition, *Africa: Whatever you Thought, Think Again*, September 2005 (Washington DC.: National Geographic, 2005), 21.

[3] http://www.bbc.co.uk/worldservice/africa/features/storyofafrica/2chapter4.shtml (accessed January 18 2003).

[4] **Cheikh Anta Diop**, *The African Origin of Civilization* (Westport: Lawrence Hill and Company Publisher, 1974), 180.

[5] People of ancient Ghana and Mali.

[6] Ellias N. **Saad**, *Social History of Timbuktu, 1400-1900: the Role of Muslim Scholars and Notables* (Illinois: Library of Congress: an Award Winning Dissertation Submitted to the Graduate School in Partial Fulfilment of the Requirements for the Degree, Doctor of Philosophy, Field of History, 1979), 15-16.

[7] **Hochschild**, p. 261.

[8] Sir Evelyn Baring was the governor of Kenya during the *Mau Mau* uprising and the British State of Emergency.

[9] Is a teachers' training college where the British colonial government had one of many assizes and raised a pair of gallows for convictions and executions of Kikuyu.

[10] David Anderson, Histories of the Hanged: the Dirty War in Kenya and the End of Empire (New York, W.W. Northon & Company Publisher, 2005), 173.

[11] Anderson, p. 78.

[12] Johnnie Cochran was an African American lawyer who was famous for defending disadvantaged people. His most famous trial was O.J. Simpson versus state of California. In that trial that he used the phrase, he would come to be best known for "If it doesn't fit, you must acquit." He died yesterday.

[1] **John Henley,** "Law on Teaching History Stirs the Ghosts of Empire," in the *Guardian* (London, England: the Guardian, April 16, 2005

[2] Walter **Rodney,** *How Europe Underdeveloped Africa* (Washington DC.: Howard University Press Publisher, 1982).

[3] Charles E. **Cobb Jr.,** "Africa in Fact: A Continent's Numbers Tell its Story," in the journal of *National Geographic*, Special Edition, *Africa: Whatever you Thought, Think Again* (Washington DC: September 2005 Issue.)

[1] Larry **Brook, Larry,** *Cities Through Time: Daily Life in Ancient and Modern Timbuktu* (Illinois: Runestone Press Publisher, 1999), 31.

[2] Brent D **Singleton,** "African Bibliophiles: Books and Libraries in Medieval Timbuktu," in the journal of *Libraries and Cultures* Vol. 39 No1. p.1., 2004.

[3] **Saad,** p. 22-3

[4] Mohammad Muaddab al-Kabari and Modibo Muhammad al-Kabari is the same person with different first names in two separate works.

[5] A non-Islamic, religious, or simply sinful person or action.

[6] Feminine for Hajji.

[7] Not that no member of my family is illiterate. I simply mean Western-style education. Those members that were not in the Western-style schools attended the madrasa. They were always around since my father owned the madrasa, which was located in our compound.

[8] He actually meant an Arab man

[1] Robert T. **Parsons,** *Religion in an African Society: a Study of the Religion of the Kono People of Sierra Leone in its Social Environment with Special Reference to the Function of Religion in that Society* (Leiden: E.J. Brill Publisher, 1964), xii-iii.

[2] Cyril P. **Foray,** *History Dictionary of Sierra Leone* (Metuchen, N.J. & London: The Scarecrow Press, Publisher, 1997), 112.

[3] **Foray,** 113.

[4] Larry **Brook, Larry,** *Cities Through Time: Daily Life in Ancient and Modern Timbuktu* (Illinois: Runestone Press Publisher, 1999), 31.

[1] Alan **Huffman,** "Tumult and Transition in 'Little America,'" (Washington DC.: Smithsoniam magazine, 2005), 47

[2] The then president of the United States.

[3] Ibid.

[4] He would later become president of the United States from 1817 to 1825. Between these years, the first shipment of freed slaves landed in Liberia to form a city that would be named after him, Monrovia.

[5] Walter **Rodney,** *How Europe Underdeveloped Africa* (Washington DC.: Howard University Press, 1982), 40.

[6] Howard W **French,** *A Continent for the Taking* (New York: Alfred A. Knope Publisher, 2004), 91.

[7] W.H.D. **Rouse,** *Great Dialogues of Plato* (New York: Penguin Putnam Publisher, 1999), 129.

[8] Late William Tolbert who Samuel Doe had killed in a coup was a father-in-law of Félix Houphouët-Boigny's daughter.

[9] Tarta **Teh,** *Still Stupid after All These Years* (http://members.aol.com/Liberia99/Still_Stupid_after_All_These.htm (accessed June 17, 2002).

[10] He was the American president with the longest limbs.

[11] **Huffman,** p. 49.

[12] Howard W. **French,** *A Continent for the Taking* (New York: Alfred A. Knope Publisher, 2004), 222.

[13] A young soldier who, with Doe, staged the 1980 coup that overthrew William Tolbert.

Notes

[1] Christopher **Andrew, and Vasili MitroKhin,** *The World was Going our Way: The KGB and the Battle for the Third World* (New York: Basic Books Publisher, 2005), 429.

[2] **LexisNexis,** "Congo: Internal Affairs and Foreign Affairs, January 1960-January 1963," in the *Confidential U.S. State Department Central Files* (Maryland: 1960-63).

[3] Madiba, **Mandela,** *Long Walk to Freedom* (New York: Back Bay Books Publisher, 1995), 295.

[4] **Andrew and Mitrokhin,** p. 428.

[5] **Adam Hochschild,** *King Leopold II's Ghost* (New York: Mariner Books Publisher, 1999), 3.

[6] **Andrew and Mitrokhin, p.** 432.

[7] Stephen R. **Weisman,** "Opening the Secret Files on Lumumba's Murder," in the journal of the Washington Post (Washington DC: the Washington Post, July 21, 2002)

[8] **Andrew and Mitrokhin, p.** 425-427.

[9] **Andrew and Mitrokhin, p.** 451.

[10] An early single-barrelled machine gun that was cooled by an outer casing containing water and a small fast ship with large guns mounted on it used for example by the coast guard. These were the two main instruments of terror in gunboat diplomacy in colonial Africa.

[11] Chinua **Achebe,** *Things Fall Apart* (New York: Anchor Books Publisher, 1994), 45.

[12] Richard **Willing, Richard,** "DNA rewrites history for African-Americans," in the USA Today http://www.usatoday.com/news/nation/2006-02-01-dna-tests_x.htm., February 1 2006.

[13] **Franz Fanon,** *The Wretched of the Earth, 254* (New York: Grove Press Publisher, 1963).

[14] **Fanon, p.** 255.

[15] **Fanon,** p. 296, 297.

[16] **Fanon,** p. 299-00.

[17] **Fanon,** p. 300.

[18] **Fanon,** p. 301.

[19] **Fanon,** p. 301.

[20] **Fanon,** p. 293.

[21] **Hochschild,** p. 111.

[22] Charlayne Hunter-Gault, "An Apology 65 Years Late," in The *NewsHour with Jim Lehrer Transcript.* (Washington:, USA, May 16, 1997). After blood tests of the volunteers, 399 men with syphilis and a control group of 201 men without the disease were chosen. But the 399 were not told they had syphilis or that they were now part of a medical experiment.

[23] **Hunter-Gault,** "An Apology 65 Years Late."

[24] Nelson Madiba **Mandela,** *Long Walk to Freedom* (New York: Back Bay Books Publisher, 1995), 122.

[25] **Mandela,** *In His Own Words* (New York: Little Brown and Company Publisher, 2003), xiii.

[26] Mandela, p. 27.

[27] **Hochschild,** p. 111.

[28] Mobutu Sese Seko was the despotic ruler of Congo then Zaire for thirty years until ill health weakened his massive mandibles from power before Laurence Kabila overthrew him in 1998.

[29] **Hochschild,** p. 88.

[30] **Hochschild,** p. 304.

[31] **Jonathan M. Fishbein,** "Phase 11B Trail to Determine the Efficacy of Oral AZT and the Efficacy of Oral Nevirapine for the Prevention of Vertical Transmission of HIV-1 Infection in Prenatal Uganda Women and Their Neonates" on *Honest Doctor.rog* (Washington DC. USA, 2003).

[32] Christopher **Lee**, "Africa - Nevirapine For AIDS Mothers: US Hid Research Concerns," in *The Washington Post* (Washington DC.: February 2 2005).

[33] **(AP Press):** an unknown source article

[34] There are reports of twins and triplets infants' offspring of the research group.

[35] Management title not listed

[36] Deputy Director, Division of AIDS, NIAID

[37] Honest Doctor.org, Today, at the National Institutes of Health upward of 1,600 managers and senior research specialists are classified as Title 42 employees. While Title 42 employees function with all of the authority and responsibilities of civil service employees, their right to pursue grievances against the government is sharply curtailed. Indeed, the government's position is that not only are Title 42 employees less than full employees, but they are also entitled to fewer constitutional protections than their civil service counterparts.

[38] A possible typo as it appears in the e-mail document.

[39] Director, Division of AIDS, NIAID

[40] Executive Officer, NIAID

[41] Director, NIAID

[42] I am a graduate of the Johns Hopkins University School of Medicine. I completed fellowships at both the National Cancer Institute and the Massachusetts General Hospital/Harvard Medical School in transplantation immunology

I pursued a career in pharmaceutical clinical research. For ten years, I served as a physician at PAREXEL International Corporation, overseeing medical safety for dozens of clinical research programs in a wide variety of therapeutic areas. In the last five of those years, four of which I was a vice president; I oversaw all medical drug development and safety activities in North America. I supervised as many as fourteen physicians and a staff of eighty clinical trials specialists situated in six different locations in the United States.

During my career with PAREXEL, one of the world's largest contract research organizations, I was involved directly or indirectly with approximately 450 clinical trials from nearly every major pharmaceutical company in almost every therapeutic area. I have also assisted in the drafting of the revised fourth edition of *New Drug Development: A Regulatory Overview* by Mark Mathieu. I am recognized internationally as an expert in the field of Good Clinical Practice or GCP.

As part of my medical training and my experience in drug development, I gained a healthy respect for the *Good Clinical Practice: Consolidated Guidance*, the bible for conducting valid, safe, and ethical research.

[43] At the time of writing this discussion in March 2005.

[44] Director of U.S. Department of Health and Human Services.

[45] CD4 blood cell count less than 250 per millimetre cube of blood.

[46] FDA. Public Health Advisory for nevirapine. Viramune.

[47] **Hochschild,** 301.

[48] Mohamed Sorie **Forna,** *Letter of Resignation to Prime Minister Siaka Stevens,* in the *Historical Document* (Freetown, Sierra Leone: 1970.

[49] David **Quammen,** "Tracing the Human Footprint," in the journal of *National Geographic,* Special Edition, *Africa: Whatever you Thought, Think Again,* September 2005 (Washington DC.: 2005), 21.

[50] Wayne **Madsen,** *Genocide and Covert Operations in Africa 1993—1999* (New York, The Edwin Mellen Press, 1999), 28.

[51] **Andrew and Mitrokhin, P** 428.

[52] **Andrew and Mitrokhin,** P. 430.

[53] **Madsen, Wayne,** p. 51.

[54] W.H.D. **Rouse,** *Great Dialogues of Plato* (New York, Penguin Putnam Publisher, 1999), 123.

Notes

[1] John Peter-**Pham**, *Liberia: Portrait of a Failed State* (New York, Reed Press Publisher, 2004), 95.

[2] Ibid.

[3] Tarta **Teh**, *Still Stupid after All These Years* http://members.aol.com/Liberia99/Still_Stupid_after_All_These.htm (accessed June 17, 2002).

[4] Wayne **Madsen**, "Covert Operations in Africa: Smoking Gun in Washington," a presentation to the (Congresswoman Ms. Cynthia McKinney's International Investigative Journalists' roundtable Conference, April 16, 2001).

[5] Wayne **Madsen**, *Genocide and Covert Operations in Africa 1993—1999* (New York: The Edwin Mellen Press, 1999), 41.

[6] **Wayne Madsen,** "Genocide and Covert Operations in Africa 1993-1999" a presentation to the (United States House of Representatives: Subcommittee on International Operations and Human Rights Committee on International relations, May 17, 2001).

[7] *African Dawn by Keita Fodeba*

(Guitar music)

Dawn was breaking. The little village, which had danced half the night to the sound of its tom-toms, was waking slowly. Ragged shepherds playing their flutes were leading their flocks down into the valley. The girls of the village with their canaries followed one by one along the winding path that leads to the fountain. In the marabout's courtyard a group of children were softly chanting in the chorus some verses from the Koran.

(Guitar music)

Dawn was breaking—dawn, the fight between night and day. But the night was exhausted and could fight no more, and slowly died. A few rays of the sun, the forerunners of this victory of the day, still hovered on the horizon, pale and timid, while the last stars gently glided under the mass of clouds, crimson like the blooming flamboyant flowers.

(Guitar music)

Dawn was breaking. And dawn at the end of the vast plain with its purple contours, the silhouette of a bent man tilling the ground could be seen, the silhouette of Naman the labourer. Each time he lifted his hoe the frightened birds rose, and flew swiftly away to find the quiet banks of the Djoliba, the great Niger River. The man's gray cotton trousers, soaked by the dew, flapped against the grass on either side. Sweating, un-resting, always bent over he worked with his hoe; for the seed had to be sown before the next rains came.

(Cora music)

Dawn was breaking, still breaking. The sparrows circled amongst

The leaves announcing the day. On the damp track leading to the plain a child, carrying his little quiver of arrows round him like a bandolier, was running breathless toward Naman. He called out: "Brother Naman, the headman of the village wants you to come to the council tree."

(Cora music)

The labourer, surprised by such a message so clearly in the morning, laid down his hoe and walked toward the village which now was shining in the beams of the rising sun. Already the old men of the village were sitting under the tree looking more solemn than ever. Beside them a man in uniform, a district guard, sat impressively, quietly smoking his pipe.

(Cora music)

Naman took his place on the sheepskin. The headman's spokesman stood up to the assembly the will of the old men: "The white men have sent a district guard to ask for a man from the village who will go to the war in their country. The chief men, after taking counsel together, have decided to send the young man who is the best representative of our race, so that he may go and give proof to the white men of that courage which has always been a feature of our *Manding*."

(Guitar music)

Naman was thus officially marked out, for every evening the village girls praised his great stature and muscular appearance in musical couplets. Gentle Kadia, his young wife, overwhelmed by then news, suddenly ceased grinding corn, put the mortar away under the barn, and without saying a word shut herself into her hut to weep over her misfortune with stifled sobs. For death had taken her first husband; and she could not believe that now the white people had taken Naman from her, Naman who was the centre of all her new-sprung hopes.

(Guitar music)

The next day, in spite of her tears and lamentations, the full-toned drumming of the war tom-toms accompanied Naman to the village's little harbour where he boarded a trawler which was going to the district capital. That night, instead of dancing in the marketplace as they usually did, the village girls came to keep watch in Naman's outer room, and there told their tales until morning around a wood fire.

(Guitar music)

Several months went by without any news of Naman reaching the village. Kadia was so worried that she went to the cunning fetish-worker from the neighbouring village. The village elders themselves held a short secret council on the matter, but nothing came of it.

(Cora music)

At last one day a letter from Naman came to the village, to Kadia's address. She was worried as to what was happening to her husband, and so that same night she came, after hours of tiring walking, to the capital of the district, where a translator read the letter to her.

Naman was in North Africa; he was well, and he asked for news of the harvest, of the feastings, the river, the dances, the council tree... in fact, for news of the entire village.

(Balafo music)

Again several months went by and everyone was once more anxious, for nothing more was heard of Naman. Kadia was thinking of going again to consult the fetish-worker when she received a second letter. Naman, after passing through Corsica and Italy, was now in Germany and was proud of having been decorated.

(Balafo music)

But the next time there was only a postcard to say that Naman had been made prisoner by the Germans. This news weighed heavily on the village. The old men held council and decided that henceforward Naman would be allowed to dance the Douga, that sacred dance of the vultures that no one who has not performed some outstanding feat is allowed to dance, that dance of the Mali emperors of which every step is a stage in the history of the Mali race. Kadia found consolation in the fact that her husband had been raised to the dignity of a hero of his country.

(Guitar music)

Time went by. A year followed another, and Naman was still in Germany. He did not write any more.

(Guitar music)

One fine day, the village headman received word from Dakar that Naman would soon be home. The mutter of the tom-toms was at once heard. There was dancing and singing till dawn. The village girls composed new songs for his home-coming, for the old men who were the devotees of the Douga spoke no more about the famous dance of the *Manding*.

(Tom-Toms)

But a month later, Corporal Mousa, a great friend of Naman's wrote a tragic letter to Kadia: "Dawn was breaking. We were at Tiaroye-sur-mer. In the course of a widespread dispute between us and our white officers from Dakar, a bullet struck Naman. He lies in the land of Senegal."

(Guitar music)

Yes; dawn was breaking. The first rays of the sun hardly touched the surface of the sea as they gilded its little foam-flecked waves. Stirred by the breeze, the palm trees gently bent their trunks down toward the ocean, as if saddened by the morning's battle. The crows came in noisy flocks to warn the neighbourhood by their cawing of the tragedy that was staining the dawn at Tiaroye with blood. And in the flaming blue sky, just above Naman's body, a huge vulture was hovering heavily. It seemed to say to him, "Naman! You have not danced that dance that is named after me. Others will dance it."

(Cora music)

Notes

[1] An RUF rebel leader, whose fighters hacked victims limbs at the wrist or above the elbow, name-branded long sleeve or short sleeve respectively.

[2] A nickname, opponents of the slave trade gave to traders and owners of slaves.

[3] Erica **Williams,** *Capitalism and Slavery* (North Carolina: The University of North Carolina Press Publisher, 1994) , 126.

[4] Ottobah Cugoano's book *Thoughts and Sentiments on the Evil of Slavery* was publish in England in 1787

[5] Or Gustavus Vassa, the English name he went by.

[6] Christopher **Fyfe,** *A History of Sierra Leone* (London: Oxford University Press, 1962), 13.

[7]**Jack Abramoff: The House That Jack Built***:* ***ttp://www.thinkprogress.org/abramof*** (accessed July 19 2006).

[8] David **Anderson,** *Histories of the Hanged: The Dirty War in Kenya and the End of Empire* (New York: W.W. Norton & Company, 2005), 203.

[9] **United Nations (2005):** "Meeting the Challenges of Unemployment in Africa," in the journal of the Economic Report on Africa 2005 (New York: United Nations), 1.

[10] David **Leigh, and David Pallister,** "Revealed: the New Scramble for Africa," in the *Guardian* newspaper (London: England, 2005).

[11]**Norman Dixon** "AFRICA: Millions for Military Aid, a Pittance for the Starving," In the journal of Green Left Weekly (Washington DC.: 2005).

[12] Jonathan A. **Peters,** "Pis Pis Pis and the January 6, 1999, Rebel Incursion," in the journal *African Studies, (*Baltimore: University of Maryland, 2005), 30.

13 An organization of former peace corps volunteer in Sierra Leone and persons interested in Sierra Leone.

14 An NGO of doctors that help countries in crisis with medical needs.

Notes

cxvi Wayne **Madsen,** *Genocide and Covert Operations in Africa 1993—1999* (New York: The Edwin Mellen Press, 1999), xxiv.

cxvii Christopher **Fyfe,** *A History of Sierra Leone* (London: Oxford University Press, 1962), 16.

cxviii Larry **Brook,** *Cities Through Time: Daily Life in Ancient and Modern Timbuktu* (Illinois: Runestone Press Publisher, 1999), 52.

cxix Ellias N. **Saad,** *Social History of Timbuktu, 1400-1900: the Role of Muslim Scholars and Notables* (Illinois: Library of Congress: an Award Winning Dissertation Submitted to the Graduate School in Partial Fulfilment of the Requirements for the Degree, Doctor of Philosophy, Field of History, 1979), 7-8.

cxx **Brook,** p. 49.

cxxi Figures are taken from the United Nation's International Labour Organization worker migration figures.

cxxii **Plato (c. 360 B.C.),** "Crito; The Prison of Socrates," *Translated by Benjamin Jowett.*

cxxiii Larry **Brook,** *Cities Through Time: Daily Life in Ancient and Modern Timbuktu* (Illinois: Runestone Press Publisher, 1999), 4.

cxxiv Robert A. **Dahl,** "The Problem of Civic Competence," in the *Journal of Democracy* (Washington DC.: Journal of Democracy, 1992), 45.

cxxv Ibid.

cxxvi Dahl's explanation: "*The problem of trustworthy surrogates.* No one can know enough to make a fully informed judgment on every issue one confronts. In order to arrive at judgments about most matters, then, everyone must rely on trusted surrogates. This is true not only of ordinary citizens but of the most highly informed scholars and experts, who in making judgments about the truth or validity of most questions invariably rely heavily on the statement of others, even within their own area of expertise. A trusted surrogate, however, may not be a trustworthy surrogate. Obviously, civic competence requires citizens to do more than look to trusted surrogates; they must also be able to tell which surrogates are worthy of trust."

[cxxvii] At the new Timbuktu International Airport (TIA), which would be hugged and shadowed by her monumental multi-storey airport complex and surrounding hotels, one would be greeted with a smack in the face by a huge golden statue of the smiling Na-Bactoo in memory of centuries of servitude. It would surpass the United Sates' Statue of Liberty in stature. She would be there, still in her symbolic servile duty, draped and veiled with a basket of wares in her grips. Engraved in the monumental proportion concrete base would read these words, "Welcome to Timbuktu: A Friendly City of Trade and Industry."

This great new city would creep from the banks of the Niger River bend in the south, deep into the earth of ancient Timbuktu, Jenne, and Kabara, all the way into the northern desert land. Her suburbs would extend into the states of Algeria and Niger. One would drive all the way into Algeria and Niger without noticing you have actually left Timbuktu proper. Southward, she would hug her formal colonial boundaries with the states of Guinea and Ivory Coast and Burkina Faso eastward. Toward the state of Mauritania, she would swallow the ancient city of Walata.

The bright sun would pierce the bright blue skies and hovering white clouds that would often be pregnant with rain above distant horizon as far as eyes can see.

Timbuktu! This brand-new city would be the capital city of the United African States (UAS). It would be unlike her ancient, colonial and postcolonial predecessors. Timbuktu would be unlike any city in the whole world. Visitors to Timbuktu would find a city of unsurpassed diversity marked by a complex society of peoples of different religious cultures and backgrounds.

Black Africans, Arab Africans, and European Africans along with Asian Africans and Indian Africans, would all work hand in hand in Timbuktu and in all other big and small cities. This great nation would become the envy of the rest of the world, especially Europe and the United States of America.

Twelve-lane asphalt highways would snake from the rain forest straight out into the earth of the desert. Driving from the Niger bend in the South, to the northern edges of the city of Timbuktu, would be in no time at nonstop cruising speed.

This great new city would always be hard at work during the days by the simple philosophy: "Business before pleasure." And business would thrive in the city. The salary structure would be well thought out—one would not find CEOs in the UAS making hundred times the ordinary workers as in the West. This would be one of the significant distinctions between market capitalism and

African communalism. There would exist in UAS the best and well-enforced wage laws in the world.

Besides the base salary and wage, UAS would structure a system that would allow special benefit workers based on family size. Education, experience, and performance would remain the primary factors for better earnings however. But the per-household count standard consideration would improve living condition for all. This would ensure outstanding family and community programs: a great nation-building community through an excellent economic system around the family.

The big tea culture would return to Timbuktu. The cafés and bars in downtown Timbuktu would serve more tea and coffee than alcohol. Such human vice as alcoholism would naturally disappear in a society of peoples of chastened moral conduct and higher work ethics. Africa would have revisited its historical culture of offering tea to guests of honour. "In ancient Timbuktu, the Tuareg offered tea, their greatest luxury, to guests of honour."

Working hours would be solemn in Timbuktu—it would be busy. People would be about business and tending to civic responsibilities, working hard, reading hard, watching the news updates, holding free political discussions, holding political meetings, and organizing peaceful demonstrations freely for their rights and concerns in a nation of civic competent citizenry.

Timbuktu would offer the finest men and women on the world stage of diplomacy. UAS would be the only nation of the world that would boast of speaking all the major languages of the world. Its diverse language citizenry is already the only good colonial legacy. And the UAS would put it into good use by having multilingual diplomats. For example, the Asian Africans—Chinese and Indians who were brought to Africa to help the colonial masters to plunder its resources—would by now have pledged committed and unsurpassed allegiance not to China and India or the formal colonial masters, but to UAS. They would be representing this great nation in Asian countries, cultures they understand well, where they would mix well with the people to stand at vantage point in diplomatic negotiations.

In the Middle East, the Arab Africans would inflict severe blows at their cousins in diplomacy on behalf of the UAS.

It would be pleasant to see the Boers dominating diplomatic missions to Europe, fighting to bring back all what had been stolen from Africa by the forebears.

Mozambique and Angola would supply outstanding men and women to represent UAS in the Portuguese and Spanish countries. People from the states of Ethiopia would engage the Italians. UAS dominance in multilateral organizations would become a butt of jealousy for Europeans. But they would have themselves to blame to have assembled such an unexpected formidable force in slavery and colonialism. It would be a payback time for Europeans to have broken Africa up into these too many states in the past for centuries for selfish reasons. All there is to be added here is "whatever goes around comes around."

The congressional mosques of Timbuktu and Jenne would become the University of Timbuktu in a modern sense of a university. The old mosques would become historical sites within the greater university settings. There would be two different campuses: the University of Timbuktu at Timbuktu and the University of Timbuktu at Jenne. Many historical artefacts about ancient Timbuktu would be stored and maintained in the old mosques. It would become the best historical university of the world. People from all over the world would come there to do, especially historical research.

Downtown Timbuktu would extend from along the banks of the Niger bend up to the beautiful port at Kabara. It would have a great view at the port of Kabara, especially at night. Hanging bridges would link the city to its well-lit suburbs on the other side of the banks of the river. From that end, first-class highways would link Timbuktu to all her western, central, and southern states. North Timbuktu also would provide a great network of highways to the northern and eastern states.

Bars, cafés, restaurants, and huge entertainment and hotel complexes would hug the Niger River banks on both sides. The flood plain would be developed into a tourist attraction infrastructure. Human activities would facilitate much rain just as in the ancient past when this community was full of life.

Once one is within the borders of the UAS, there would be no local checkpoints in this great nation. There would be an international airport in every state. Freedom of movement would be at its best in UAS. Domestic airports and flights would "grow on trees" in the UAS. There would be flights and rails to its major cities around the clock.

Business travellers would find it very easy to navigate the UAS. But they would be warned to leave their three-piece suits back in Europe and the United States since they will be of no use in Africa. Sunshine and rainfall would be best all year round. Sometimes it would shine and rain at once, and it would be beautiful.

The House of Mansa (State House) would be a huge monument that would stand on a vast land from where the major streets would originate and stretch out east, west, north, and south. It would have four wings, each one of them would symbolize one of the four major faiths of the people of the UAS. The far left wing would have domes and arches like the congressional mosques of ancient Timbuktu and Jenne, the near left would be shaped like the synagogue of Ethiopia, the near right would be one huge gazebo shaped for traditionalism, and the far right would have domes and arches like a church. One could imagine reporters making joke of this in the future that "next the Mansa would have to grow some grass outside the House of Mansa for Buddha's cow to graze." Indeed Buddha's people would have great freedom to practice Buddhism in this great nation or whatever religion anyone would want to practice.

Press freedom in UAS would be the best in the world. The leaders would even brush off extreme seditious comments against them and the government to go about their daily business of running a nation.

These huge stone walls, domes, and arches of the House of Mansa would make a statement that this

Timbuktu unlike her predecessors would stay forever in glory. On the left, there would be another monument, which would be the House of Koi and Mondyo (House of Legislature). The Koi would be the upper house and the Mondyo the lower house. There would be, at least, two Kois per state. Depending on the size and population, a state could have as many as four Kois. The states of Nigeria, South Africa, Congo, Egypt, and Algeria would be examples of such states with four Kois. There would be as many Mondyos per state as there would be districts in the state, where every Mondyo would represent a district in the lower house of Mondyos.

Every state would have a Farma (a state government) and a house of Koi and Mondyo at state level just as would be in the UAS central government. The heads of the state governments would be the Farmas (governors). To the right of the House of Mansa would be the House of Jurists (Supreme Court) that would house the Joint Supreme Jurists. They would be fifteen in numbers, and they would be the highest jurists of the judicial organ of this great nation. These men of wisdom and virtue, who would be appointed by the Mansa and confirmed by both houses of representatives, would be headed by the Supreme Jurists' Jurist who would be equivalent to the supreme chief justice in the United States of America.

Two blocks east of these well-located three independent organs of the government of the UAS—the executive, the legislature, and the judiciary would be the House of Askias, which would be the department of defence. It would face north, away from all the civilian departments. This will be a psychological and symbolical reinforcement of the constitution that the House of Askias would have no business in politics except to vote and support a political party as individual civic obligation. It would house the Joint Askias of Defense. They would be nine great men of courage and unsurpassed patriotism who would be led by the Askia the Great as guardians of the nation.

Thus, there would be many peaceful democratic elections in this great nation regardless of its many political parties, diverse groups, and diverse interests. But it would be exceptional the way the people would be working toward one peaceful and democratic society. There would be many political parties. But there would be criteria as to which once make it to the final elections.

This city of Timbuktu would be a perfect example of a great seat of a government; there would be a mushroom of ministerial buildings called House of Farma. But these Houses of Farma would be different in the sense that instead of saying, for instance, the Farma of Sierra Leone as would be in the title of a governor, they would be called the Farma for Family and Community Development in the case of the ministers. He would work directly with the state farmer of Sierra Leone and all the farmers in all the fifty-five states.

Great cities would rise all over the nation; its tourist industry state of Egypt in the north would be a phenomenon for tourism. Morocco's big historical cities would make huge profit through tourism. The oil drilling states of Algeria, Libya, Sudan, Tunisia, Angola, Gabon, and Nigeria would be big contributors to this vibrant economy of UAS. The state of Mali, the location of modern Timbuktu would become the federal ground. The government would lure many new businesses and industries to the surrounding states to avoid congestion in Mali. Regardless of the booming economy and metropolis that would emerge in Timbuktu, great efforts would be put into avoiding congestion.

Unlike the United Sates' Washington DC residents whose residents do not have representation, Malians would have full representation. They would have two Kois and Mondyos who would represent all its districts. The state Farma would run the state of Mali. In fact, Mali would be making billions and billions of $û$ (wudi [the local currency]) from taxing the central government for its entire establishment in Timbuktu. Wudi would become the most widely accepted currency in the world for international trade over the U.S. dollar and the European euro.

The states of Algeria, Niger, Burkina Faso, Ivory Coast, Guinea. Gambia, Senegal, and Mauritania capitals would have all become great metropolis. The new crude oil deposits of a small state northwest of Mauritania called W. Sahara would boost its contribution to the UAS economy. The diamond mines of the state of Sierra Leone would have turned Freetown, its state capital, into the new Brussels second only to the state of South Africa.

Diamond cutting and polishing businesses would mushroom in the state capital city of Freetown and all the towns in the state of Sierra Leone. The UAS central government would redirect Fourah Bay College's focus on geological and mining studies.

The state of Chad would not be a vast waste desert land anymore; industries would pop up there in fears competition for location and localization. The Stanley and Acosombo falls of the states of Congo and Ghana would supply electricity to all of Africa, including its remotest villages.

Plantation farming in the states of Ethiopia, Eritrea, Uganda, Kenya, Rwanda, Burundi, Cameroon, and Central Africa would all embark on mechanized farming. Gone would be the days of land tenure system in Africa. This nation would now be festooned with vast plains of high-tech agriculture.

Business activities in the diamond industry, especially in the state of South Africa, would flourish. There would be so much diamonds coming from the state of Angola as well. Botswana, Angola, Sierra Leone, and South Africa would be producing so much diamonds that they would have to be placed under check to avoid the plunging of the price of diamonds on the world market. But the central government would be competent enough to control the market—the Farma for Mining would divert Angola's focus more on oil production than diamond mining. The UAS would control the World Bank—the owner of the money must speak louder, and the Mansa's voice would be echoing loud over the microphones of international roundtable conferences.

The wild plains of South Africa would supply all the grains that would be needed in UAS and some more for export to European countries. In fact, the central government would encourage the state of South African farmers to produce more grains to help with reducing poverty and starvation in the world.

143

The states of Botswana, Namibia, Madagascar, Somalia, Zambia, Congo (Kinshasa), Zimbabwe, Togo, Benin, Liberia, and Malawi would all been bashing in the glory in the service industry. Exploitation of their natural resources would be put on hold for future generations. Many other states would have so much to offer the central government would have to make such a wise decision to put a check on how the land would be exploited.

The states of São Tomé and Príncipe, Seychelles, Guinea-Bissau, Djibouti, Comoros, and Cape Verde would all contribute and share the prosperity evenly in UAS.

Now let us envision what would become of the bulldog—the state of Nigeria. It would become the commerce and manufacturing industry of the world. Big machines, trucks, and cars would be tubing out of its assembly lines like candy bars. Science and technology would be at its best. The agro industry would be supported heavily by the science and technology, which would reduce the exploitation of the land and subsequently the natural resources.

When you say manufacturing in the world, you would be saying Lagos. Important, the Mansa of UAS would put a stop to production of minerals that would be used for the manufacturing of weapons of mass destruction in a determination to clamp down on such material. The UAS would have no enemies, but friends through the fine works of these great men and women of its diplomatic core. The UAS would not interfere with the affairs of any other nation. Thus, the UAS would not be under threat from no other nation.

This is no utopia, it is possible.

Bibliography

Achebe, Chinua (1994): *Things Fall Apart* (New York, Anchor Books Publisher).

_____(1994): *No Longer at Ease* (New York, Anchor Books Publisher).

_____(1987): *Anthills of the Savannah* (New York, Anchor Books Publisher).

Ahmadu, Fuambai (2000): "Rites and Wrongs: An Insider/Outsider Reflects on Power and Excision", in the *Journal of Female "Circumcision" in Africa* (Boulder, Colorado, USA).

_____(2005): *Cutting the Anthill: The Matrilineal Foundations of Female and Male Circumcision Rituals among the Mandinka of Brikama, The Gambia* (Dissertation Submitted to the Graduate School in Partial Fulfillment of the Requirements for the Degree, Doctor of Philosophy, Field of Anthropology, London School of Economics).

Amadiume, I. (1997): *Reinventing Africa: Matriarchy, Religion and Culture* (London, Zed Books Ltd publisher).

Andrew, Christopher and Vasili MitroKhin (2005): *The World was Going our Way: The KGB and the Battle for the Third World* (New York, Basic Books Publisher).

Arnold, Caroline (1992): *Camel* (New York, Morrow Junior Books Publisher).

Anderson, David (2005): *Histories of the Hanged: The Dirty War in Kenya and the End of Empire* (New York, W.W. Norton & Company).

Brook, Larry (1999): *Cities Through Time: Daily Life in Ancient and Modern Timbuktu* (Illinois, Runestone Press Publisher).

Butler, Samuel (Translated) (1999): *Homer: The Iliad & The Odyssey*, (New York, Barnes & Nobles Books Publisher).

Cobb, Charles E Jr. (2005): "Africa in Fact: A Continent's Numbers Tell its Story," in the journal of *National Geographic*, Special Edition, *Africa: Whatever you Thought, Think Again*, September 2005 Issue.

Dahl, Robert A. (1992): "The Problem of Civic Competence", in the *Journal of Democracy* (Washington DC, USA).

Dawood, N.J. (2000): *The Koran with Parallel Arabic Text* (London, Penguin Books Publisher).

Diamond, Jared (2005): "The Shape of Africa," in the journal of *National Geographic*, Special Edition, *Africa: Whatever you Thought, Think Again*, September 2005 Issue.

Diop, Cheikh Anta (1974): *The African Origin of Civilization* (Westport, Lawrence Hill and Company Publisher).

Dixon Norman (2005): "AFRICA: Millions for Military Aid, a Pittance for the Starving," In the journal of Green Left Weekly (Washington, USA).

Dobler, Lavinia and William A. Brown (1965): *Great Rulers of the African Past* (New York, Garden City Publisher).

Ebenstein, William and Alan Ebenstein (2000): *Great Political Thinkers: Plato to the Present* (Belmont, Wadsworth Group Publisher).

Fage, J.D. (2002): *A History of Africa* (London, Routledge Publisher).

Fanon, Frantz (1963): *The Wretched of the Earth* (New York, Grove Press Publisher).

Fishbein, Jonathan M. (2003): "Phase 11B Trail to Determine the Efficacy of Oral AZT and the Efficacy of Oral Nevirapinefor the Prevention of Vertical Transmission of HIV-1 Infection in Prenatal Uganda Women and Their Neonates" on *Honest Doctor.rog* (Washington DC. USA).

Foray, Cyril P. (1997): *History Dictionary of Sierra Leone* (Metuchen, N.J. & London, The Scarecrow Press, Publisher).

Forna, Mohamed Sorie (1970): *Letter of Resignation to Prime Minister Siaka Stevens*, (Sierra Leone Historical Document).

Fyfe, Christopher (1962): *A History of Sierra Leone* (London, Oxford University Press).

Goodsmith, Lauren (1993): *Children of Mauritania: Days in the desert and by the River Shore* (Minneapolis, Carol Rhoda Books Publisher).

Henley, John (April 16, 2005): "Law on Teaching History Stirs the Ghosts of Empire", in the *Guardian,* (London, England).

Hochschild, Adam (1999): *King Leopold II's Ghost* (New York, Mariner Books Publisher).

Hunter-Gault, Charlayne (May 16, 1997): "An Apology 65 Years Late", in The *NewsHour with Jim Lehrer Transcript.* (Washington, USA).

Hunwick, John (1999): *Timbuktu and the Songhai Empire: Al-Sadi's Tarikh al-sudan Down to 1613 and other Contemporary Documents* (Leiden, Brill Publisher).

Kabba, Karamoh (2002): *A Mother's Saga: An Account of the Rebel War in Sierra Leone* (Washington, USA, Universal Publishers).

_____ (2004): *Lion Mountain: A Perilous Evolution of the Dens* (Baltimore, Publish American Publisher).

Koslow, Philip (1995): *Mali: Crossroads of Africa* (New York, Chelsea House publishers Publisher).

Lee, Christopher (February 2, 2005): "Africa - Nevirapine For AIDS Mothers: US Hid Research Concerns" in *The Washington Post* (Washington DC. USA).

Leigh, David and David Pallister (2005): "Revealed: the New Scramble for Africa", in the *Guardian* newspaper (London, England).

LexisNexis (1960-1963): "Congo: Internal Affairs and Foreign Affairs, January 1960-January 1963" in the *Confidential U.S. Sate Department Central Files* (Maryland, USA).

Madsen, Wayne (1999): *Genocide and Covert Operations in Africa 1993—1999* (New York, The Edwin Mellen Press).

_____ (April 6, 2001): "Covert Operations in Africa: Smoking Gun in Washington" a presentation to the (Congresswoman Ms. Cynthia McKinney's International Investigative Journalists' roundtable Conference).

_____ (May 17, 2001): "Genocide and Covert Operations in Africa 1993-1999" a presentation to the (United States House of Representatives: Subcommittee on International Operations and Human Rights Committee on International relations).

Mandela, Nelson Madiba (1995): Long Walk to Freedom (New York, Back Bay Books Publisher).

_____(2003): *In His Own Words* (New York, Little Brown and Company Publisher).

Mann, Kenny (1996): *Ghana, Mali, Songhai: The Western Sudan. African Kingdoms of the Past* (New Jersey, Dillon Press Publisher).

Orwell, George (1954): *Animal Farm* (New York, Longman Press Publisher).

Pakenham, Thomas (2003): *The Scramble for Africa: White Man's Conquest of the Dark Continent From 1876 to 1912* (New York, Perennial Publisher).

Parsons, Robert T. (1964): *Religion in an African Society: a Study of the Religion of the Kono People of Sierra Leone in its Social Environment with Special Reference to the Function of Religion in that Society* (Leiden, E.J. Brill Publisher).

Peters, Jonathan A. (2005): "Pis Pis Pis and the January 6, 1999, Rebel Incursion" in the journal *African Studies University of Maryland,* Baltimore, USA.

Pham, John-Peter (2004): *Liberia: Portrait of a Failed State* (New York, Reed Press Publisher).

Plato (c. 360 B.C.): "Crito; The Prison of Socrates", *Translated by Benjamin Jowett.*

Quammen, David (2005): "Tracing the Human Footprint," in the journal of *National Geographic*, Special Edition, *Africa: Whatever you Thought, Think Again*, September 2005 Issue.

Rochegude, Anne (1985): *Tuareg Boy: My Village in the Sahara* (New Jersey, Silver Burdett Publisher).

Rodney, Walter (1982): *How Europe Underdeveloped Africa* (Washington DC. Howard University Press Publisher).

Rouse, W.H.D. (1999): *Great Dialogues of Plato* (New York, Penguin Putnam Publisher).

Saad, Ellias N. (1979): *Social History of Timbuktu, 1400-1900: the Role of Muslim Scholars and Notables* (Illinois, Library of Congress: an Award Winning Dissertation Submitted to the Graduate School in Partial Fulfilment of the Requirements for the Degree, Doctor of Philosophy, Field of History).

Sampson, Anthony (1999): *Mandela: The Authorized Biography* (New York, Alfred A. Knope Publisher).

Singleton, Brent D. (2004): "African Bibliophiles: Books and Libraries in Medieval Timbuktu," in the journal of *Libraries and Cultures* Vol. 39 No1.

Stanley, Henry M. (1988): *Through the Dark Continent* (New York, Dover Publications, Publisher).

_____(1874): *How I Found Livingstone* (New York, Vivisphere Publisher).

_____(2001): *The Autobiography of Sir Henry Morton Stanley: The Making of the 19th-century Explorer* (New York, Narrative Press Publisher).

Strong, Roy (1998): *Britain: A People's history* (London, Pimlico Publisher).

Teh, Tarta (2002): *Still Stupid after All These Years* (http://members.aol.com/Liberia99/Still_Stupid_after_All_Th ese.htm).

United Nations (2005): "Meeting the Challenges of Unemployment in Africa," in the journal of the Economic Report on Africa 2005.

Weisman, Stephen R. (July 21, 2002): "Opening the Secret Files on Lumumba's Murder," in the journal of The Washington Post.

Williams, Eric (1994): *Capitalism and Slavery* (North Carilina, The University of North Carolina Press Publisher).

Willing, Richard (February 01 2006): "DNA rewrites history for African-Americans" in USA TODAY http://www.usatoday.com/news/nation/2006-02-01-dna-tests_x.htm.

www.ingramcontent.com/pod-product-compliance
Lightning Source LLC
Chambersburg PA
CBHW031849090426
42741CB00005B/417